SNOW CAMP
NORTH CAROLINA

SNOW CAMP
NORTH CAROLINA

➺ J. TIMOTHY ALLEN ➺

Charleston   London

THE
History
PRESS

Published by The History Press
Charleston, SC 29403
www.historypress.net

Copyright © 2013 by J. Timothy Allen
All rights reserved

First published 2013

Manufactured in the United States

ISBN 978.1.60949.941.9

Library of Congress CIP data applied for.

In memory of Sarah Kimball (1926–2010), the "Mayor of Snow Camp."

CONTENTS

Preface and Acknowledgements   9
Introduction   13

Snow Camp: The Beginnings   19
The John Allen House and the Randolph Coble House   25
Cane Creek Friends Quaker Meeting   31
Spring Friends Quaker Meeting   37
The American Revolution   45
Churches in Snow Camp   63
Industry   73
Early Education   87
Sylvan School   91
The Pleasant Hill Temperance Society   99
Slavery and the Underground Railroad   103
Freedom's Hill Wesleyan Church   111
Micajah McPherson   115
Sports   125
What to Do in Snow Camp   133

Conclusion   145
Bibliography   147
Index   151
About the Author   159

PREFACE AND ACKNOWLEDGEMENTS

I moved to Snow Camp in 1997. Ever since then I have heard a story or two from my neighbors about various incidents in this part of lower Alamance County (or LA, as some people say). Once in a while, I came across an article or found a section of a book that provided more illumination to this village. Following my inner historian, I began to collect these stories and file them away. While writing my history of Spring Friends Meeting in Snow Camp, I ran across more stories about the area. They did not really belong in the Spring Friends history, so I filed them away for another time. Soon I began putting together a history of Freedom's Hill Wesleyan Church, which used to be in Snow Camp until it was eventually moved to Southern Wesleyan University in Central, South Carolina. Its history cannot be understood without some knowledge of Snow Camp. Finally realizing that I had more information about Snow Camp than I did on the Freedom's Hill Church, I sent a query to The History Press, and the rest, as they say, is history (pun intended).

Writing a history of one's own town is fun and yet precarious. There is a sense of pride among the locals as they recall the past of their ancestors or tidbits from their lives. Some of this history is anecdotal and therefore not necessarily factual; indeed, sometimes there are several accounts of the same event or person. Some information is reliable and based on solid research and facts. For the tellers of the tales, it carries some importance and less validity. Thus, I understand the value placed on each vignette in the following pages.

With this in mind, there are certain restrictions that historians must abide by when writing history. First, there are the editorial guidelines that the writer must follow. Only a certain number of pages or words can be submitted. Next, there are limitations on how many pictures can be incorporated into the text. I could have included plenty more in this book, but The History Press focuses on history, not pictures. Last, some stories carry so much baggage that, while they would add to the overall history, they are better left unsaid. With all of these limitations in mind, tough decisions had to be made concerning what went into this book. I focused on history first and anecdotes second in order to provide a broad and general history. I used anecdotes sparingly to add some life to the historical stories.

Sources are always key to the historian. Sometimes a chance conversation led to an anecdote or a collection of stories. Sometimes I relied on friends. Oftentimes I was alerted to a person in the area who knew about so-and-so. Thus, a call was made. In other instances, calls, e-mails and letters were sent out, only to receive nothing in return. Once I was told by a potential interviewee that it would be a while because the corn and peas had come in and needed to be put up. Thus, items that would have been very illustrative were left behind for another day. I hope folks will understand if they deem their part of the history of Snow Camp is not in the following pages.

Organization was difficult here. Should I write a chronological narrative of Snow Camp or look at its history by subject? The former is often difficult to follow, so I chose the latter. Thus, there is some overlapping of the stories.

When dealing with anecdotes, there are the possibilities that facts contradict other facts or that memories are not as accurate as the bearer of the tale would like to think. Even scholarly sources will disagree on details. And sometimes the historian has to make an educated guess. In essence, accuracy has been the goal. The reader will have to attest to the success of the writer and the veracity of the information.

Last, when I initially began writing this story, I included endnotes to indicate which author I was citing. As I wrote, I realized that, while of importance to the professional historian, these notations would be cumbersome to the general reader. Thus, where a direct quote is made, I have listed the source in the text. Otherwise, the reader can refer to the bibliography at the end of the book for more exploration of specific topics. I relied heavily on Carole Watterson Troxler and William Murray Vincent's *Shuttle and Plow* for historical background and specific information. I am indebted to them and hope I have not gone beyond the bounds of the proper use of sources. Scholars of this region will know well the works that I used; the general reader will be either amazed or bored with my "erudition."

I would like to thank the following for their help in this project: Nancy and Buddy Aldridge; Karen Thompson; the staff at the Alamance Battleground State Historic Site; Laurie Smith (a former student) and William Murray Vincent of the Alamance County Museum; Kyle Kimball; John Allen, who read the final draft of this book; George Walls (good corndog!); Dacie Moon (now deceased); James Wilson of the Snow Camp Outdoor Theatre; Pastor Mark Tope and Cane Creek Quaker Meeting; the staff at Sylvan Elementary School; Dr. Carole Watterson Troxler, who read a rough draft of this book; Natalie Maness; Bobbie Teague; Dan Perry; Cindy Sydnor; the staff at May Memorial Library in Burlington; Marion and Marjorie Teague; Joe Bill and Jane Lindley; Floyd Wicker; Marilyn Fogleman; Bryan Wilson; and Pat Morgan. I have many more names on my list, but they will have to wait until volume two for their turn. Banks Smither, my editor at The History Press, has been most gracious throughout this project.

Finally, when we moved to Snow Camp in 1997, we brought with us our first rescue, Barnie Cat. Barnie ruled Sylvan Road for twelve years before retiring to the inside of our house. While I was writing this book, Barnie checked on me once in a while. After a good petting, he would wander off until I needed assistance again. Sadly, on the day I finished the manuscript, we had to put Barnie to sleep. I am going to miss you, my friend. Thanks for the memories.

INTRODUCTION

Two stories set the stage for a history of Snow Camp. Sometime in the mid-1700s, wandering hunters from Pennsylvania came south in search of game and perhaps excitement. They were the first white inhabitants of this area. Caught off guard by a sudden and ferocious snow- and ice storm, they made camp and rode out the winter tempest. Once the storm cleared, they continued their hunt, and after some time, they returned to the scene of their initial encampment. Much of the snow had melted, and the stumps of the trees they had cut down stood high above the ground. "Snow Camp" seemed an appropriate name for the emergency haven of the hunters. While the designation may have been more of a joke or a legendary—indeed, mythical—recollection of a dangerous time in the lives of the hunters, the appellation is now spoken with a sense of pride.

The second story goes like this: in the 1800s, a traveler stopped at a blacksmith's shop that seemed to be in the middle of nowhere. "Say, can you tell me where Snow Camp is?" the stranger asked. The blacksmith answered, "Well, I reckon you're standin' in the middle of it." Not much has changed since then.

Snow Camp is not a town. Never has been. On a map it is a dot in the road, literally an intersection with a blinking caution light. Viewed from a satellite, it is nearly all pastures and woods. No large parking lots or interstates detract from the scene. If you zoom in, you will see that Snow Camp proper consists of a store, a post office, a fire department, two restaurants and an outdoor theater. After I describe Snow Camp, people stand back in wonder, as if they have met someone who lives in the austerity of a late 1800s Appalachian village. "Where do you shop? How far is it to the nearest Walmart? What do you *do* in Snow Camp?" Today, in our fast-paced world of interstates, malls and drive-through food options, most people cannot conceive of a place as tiny as Snow Camp. Indeed, we are smaller than the fictitious Mayberry of *The Andy Griffith Show.*

Two things come to mind as you visit the place and people of Snow Camp: history and initiative. History is everywhere. There are nine historical markers within a few miles of one another that recall significant events, people and buildings. If you look farther than Snow Camp into southern Alamance County and northern Randolph County, you can find even more plaques that recall events and people directly related to Snow Camp. From the historian's perspective, Snow Camp is larger than it looks. Much larger.

Once you begin digging into the history, you begin to see just how feisty, innovative and thrifty Snow Campians have been through the centuries, demonstrated by mills, stores, patents, plank roads, new and innovative educational approaches, batteries before electricity, telephone companies, movie production and more. The people of Snow Camp have been can-do problem solvers since that first snow way back when. Snow Camp is not a sleepy little town at all.

Snow Camp was settled in 1749 by Quakers and other pioneers who came looking for cheap land. Its history usually centers on the Quakers, who quickly formed Cane Creek Friends Quaker Meeting and have worshiped here ever since. But other hearty and ambitious settlers arrived here as well. Germans and Scots-Irish were the most notable. Claims were staked, houses were built, livelihoods were carved out of the clay and woods and children were born. And soon other houses of worship emerged.

Snow Camp played two minor roles in the Revolutionary War, and both events occurred in 1781. First, British general Lord Cornwallis's weary and wounded soldiers rested here for two days just above the old Dixon mill and next to Cane Creek Meeting after their battle at Guilford Courthouse. A few months afterward, the Battle of Lindley's Mill, also known as the Battle of Snow Camp, was fought a few miles to the east.

Just before the Civil War, a small group of ardent antislavery Christians formed a new denomination, the Southern Wesleyan Church, in Snow Camp. They risked their lives for the sake of freedom for slaves.

Snow Camp was also part of the Underground Railroad, the clandestine system of trails and safe houses that helped runaway slaves reach freedom north of the "Jordan River," also known as the Ohio River. While information is still sketchy, there were probably at least four safe places for slaves to rest on their journey to freedom.

The settlers of Snow Camp were very concerned about the education of their children. Small schools abounded in the early 1800s, but one still remains: Sylvan School. Built just after the Civil War, Sylvan School was a pioneer in education in the state and continues that tradition today.

And these are just the events remembered on a few historical markers.

Before we can explore the rich past of Snow Camp, we need to know where it is. Snow Campians disagree on the reach of their community. Even locals are quick to ask just how far Snow Camp goes. The boundaries seem muddy, like Cane Creek after a gully-washer rain. Ride eight miles to the east on Greensboro–Chapel Hill Road, and you come to the Eli Whitney community, with a Snow Camp zip code. Yet, just two miles southeast away from the Snow Camp post office, addresses bear the Liberty zip code. So where does Snow Camp begin and end? Perhaps Snow Camp is more a state of mind.

Why is this important? The size of a community often says a lot about it. It is one thing to be a small village and have a milling operation and foundry. It is quite another to have an "industrial complex," as longtime resident John Allen described it, in a small community that rivals those of small cities. This was the case in the mid-1800s into the very early 1900s. One example is this: the Snow Camp Woolen Mill paid its workers a dollar a day, while mills in the nearby city of Burlington paid half that. What is the "official" population of Snow Camp? According to the 2012 census, it is over six thousand residents. So the size and population of Snow Camp vary depending on whom you ask and where you look. Paul McBane said it best: Snow Camp is as big as New York City, just with less people.

The one constant in the history of Snow Camp is that it has never been more than a small community. One word that arises again and again is "village." While signs of progress emerge within miles around it— nearby Eli Whitney (just eight miles east) now has a Dollar General, and Liberty (nine miles south) has a Walmart Express—Snow Camp seems ignored by modernity. But the folks of Snow Camp do not seem to mind. Today it lies in the southern portion of Alamance County, approximately sixteen miles south of both Graham and Burlington. Greensboro and Chapel Hill are both about twenty-five miles away to the west and east, respectively. As noted, the small town of Liberty is just south, and fifteen miles southeast is the town of Siler City, home of "Aunt Bea" of *The Andy Griffith Show*.

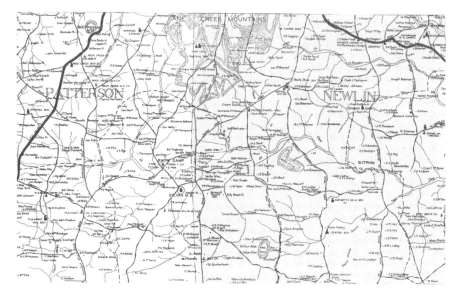

This 1928 map by Spoon, Lewis and Camp, engineers, reveals many of the places noted in this book: Oakdale (far left middle), Pleasant Hill (bottom far left), Rock Creek (above PATTERSON), "colored" school (top middle, below the word CREEK), Center (bottom middle), Bowden (middle right), Sylvan High School (lower middle). A "Baptising Hole" is just below the colored school. Churches include Rock Creek Methodist (immediately above PATTERSON), Pleasant Union (above Pleasant Hill School), Pleasant Hill Church (to the right of Pleasant Hill School), Bethlehem Holiness Church (below Sylvan High School, just above the county line), Cane Creek Friends (under SNOW CAMP), Freedom's Hill Wesleyan Church (just southwest of Sylvan School), an unknown church (by the colored school), Bethel Methodist and school (to the left of NEWLIN), Burnette's Chapel and school (southeast of SUTPHIN), Spring Friends Meeting (far right middle). Stores dot all over the map. A copper mine is marked (middle top, just southeast of MOUNTAINS). Gold was also mined in the area. *Courtesy of the Alamance County Historical Museum.*

Snow Camp is softly rolling hills with many pastures bounded by barbed wire or electric fences, tree-lined creeks and hardwood forests. Drive through Snow Camp in the fall and a palette of colors greets you at nearly every turn. In the spring, it becomes a green heaven as trees and early crops signal the new season. Perhaps the most notable and beautiful geological sight is Cane Creek. Its waters have turned many a turbine in mills throughout Snow Camp's history. It may even be the grave of British cannon or gold. The skyline is punctuated by Bass Mountain, really more like a hill. It is part of the Cane Ridge Mountains, and according to some, it may be part of the oldest mountain range in the world. Need more info on the best places to stop and look in Snow Camp? Just ask one of the many cyclists, motor and pedal, who ride through here every weekend.

Snow Camp is an amalgam of opposites. There are mobile homes and McMansions. Old farmhouses dating over one hundred years and now covered with vinyl siding contrast with new brick homes. You may get behind a rusty Massey-Ferguson tractor with years of grease and oil on it or a new, bright green John Deere. A clean-as-a-whistle Mercedes may be stuck behind a dented and dirty farm truck as the driver putts along checking out the newborn calves down the road. There are fresh pastures with shiny and taut electric wire and barely weathered posts and old ones with barbed wire nailed to seemingly ancient but still resilient cedar posts. Residents with generations of Snow Camp pedigree in their blood worry about the new influx of "foreigners" who speak in strange, unfamiliar (as in non-southern) accents. Old forests and grazing lands familiar to the memories of the older generation are now the houses and manicured lawns of newcomers.

While most of the Snow Camp population commutes to jobs in the towns and cities named above, Snow Camp is still a bucolic farming community. Trees, pastures, fields, ponds and tractors are everywhere. Round bales of hay stand guard in fields. Milk and beef cattle, chicken houses, goats and barns old and new are readily apparent, and wheat, corn, soybeans, hay and even cotton are the major crops. Several local vegetable stands arise every summer around the community, and occasional signs by the roads advertise eggs for sale.

Snow Camp is like any other small community. The center is the local gas station, affectionately known for years as the Snow Camp Raygo. Inside you can find groceries, hardware and plumbing and electrical supplies as well as fishing worms and hoop cheese and crackers. Don't forget to buy your lottery ticket! A lot of instantly rich folks are glad they stopped in Snow Camp. Locals sit on the bench outside the store and solve the problems of the community, nation and world, and occasionally the Girl Scouts or Boy Scouts sell cookies and doughnuts to the customers. Weekend cyclists, in their colorful tight shorts and shirts, provide a unique contrast to the farmers and their dirty work clothes and boots as both pause there for drinks and a brief rest. A small post office just next door serves the community, and the local fire station down the road a bit dutifully takes care of the citizens.

There are two eateries: Yesterday's Grill, constructed out of a renovated barn, has been serving up delicious food since 1999. Just a mile away is Ye Olde Country Kitchen, the fare of which has been featured on North Carolina Public Television. Stop by and look at all the Coca-Cola antiques and John Deere collectibles. Next door to the Country Kitchen is the Snow Camp Outdoor Theatre. Each season it features two major productions.

The Sword of Peace is a drama about the local Quaker resistance to the American Revolution, and the play *Pathway to Freedom* retells the story of the Underground Railroad in Snow Camp. The theater features one Broadway show and one children's production each season as well.

Another centerpiece of Snow Camp is Sylvan School. Begun in 1866 after the Civil War, it has been an academy and high school and now is an elementary school, complete with a new health clinic. Behind the school is the ballpark. Sports have been a part of Snow Camp for one hundred years. Baseball and basketball were the only sports played at Sylvan School, and today that tradition continues in the community. In the Sylvan gym, Michael Jordan wannabes shoot the jumper. On the baseball field, players go for the home run.

Once a year, the Original Hollywood Horror Show sets up for another scary Halloween season. Run by two makeup artists who worked on the *Star Trek* series and nearly two hundred other major productions, it has sent many a muscle-bound farm boy running for his life!

Twice a year, there is a bluegrass festival in Snow Camp. Formerly known as the Bass Mountain Music Festival, the Lil John's Mountain Music Festival draws major talent every year. You can also walk the links at Sourwood Forest Golf Course. Despite the initial Quaker population, churches representing many denominations can be found in the Snow Camp area. Baptists, Methodists, Christians, Wesleyans, Quakers, African Methodist Episcopal and United Church of Christ are the predominant congregations.

There are two major holiday celebrations in Snow Camp: the Christmas and July Fourth parades. Each features old tractors of many colors, antique cars, horses, four-wheelers, winning sports teams and local scout troops on decorated farm trailers, floats and the occasional politician. Sirens wail from the shiny, polished red firetrucks as the long line of participants cruise the one-mile trek from Sylvan School around by the theater and back again. Children leap for candy thrown by the participants and then all gather at the school ballpark for games and food.

I attended a conference recently that featured a noted Quaker pastor. When he found out that I had written a history of Spring Friends Quaker Meeting and was working on a history of Snow Camp, we struck up a conversation. As it turned out, he was from Danville, Indiana. Many of his meeting members' ancestors originally hailed from Snow Camp. And, as luck would have it, his family came from here as well. Snow Camp is much larger than it looks.

There is more to this sleepy community than it seems—much more! And it begins around AD 1750.

SNOW CAMP

The Beginnings

Before the white man arrived in the area, Indians roamed several trails that early pioneers and later settlers called "trading paths." Early accounts recall wigwams and what one settler, William Braxton, called "engine huts"—that is, small buildings built by local Indians. The major route ran from Hillsboro to the western Piedmont, then known as the backcountry of North Carolina, yet many branches broke away to the south. Most of these were just north and west of Snow Camp, but by 1775, one major trading path coursed through the area.

Older histories often depict the lands inhabited by the Native Americans in the eastern portion of America as deep and dark wooded forests with dense thickets all around. This was generally the case as the early settlers of Snow Camp appeared in the mid-1700s. But prior to that, Indians had cleared some lands for farming. The hearty souls who traveled the paths of the Piedmont in the 1600s discovered that Indians—the Sissipahaw and Shakory were the closest—had cleared much of the land for farming. During harvest time, the natives took crops of grains back to bark houses and granaries. One hundred years later, in Hawfields, which was about twenty miles northeast of Snow Camp, Scotch Presbyterians discovered the area was cleared by Indians for farming. Today, local legends recall that there were two Indian graves on or near the Sword of Peace Outdoor Theatre land.

Still, travelers in the heavily wooded areas of the Snow Camp territory often complained of a gloom that pervaded the dark, densely forested lands.

Game was abundant, as one would expect. Bartering between the white pioneers and the Indians regularly took place, and relations were favorable. By the end of the 1600s, the Indians were accustomed to seeing trains of settlers with loaded wagons creeping along the dusty or muddy pathways. By 1800, some Indians would intermarry with the new settlers, especially African Americans toward the eastern portion of Snow Camp.

By the mid-1700s, Scots-Irish and German immigrants, mostly from Pennsylvania and Virginia, began settling the Piedmont area, including Snow Camp in what was then Orange County. The Scots-Irish looked for lands that were like those of home, as most immigrants in this time did. They found what they were looking for in the nearly unforested portion called Hawfields. The land fit their farming style, which featured free-ranging stock.

At the same time, other folks were looking for new lands on which to farm and raise their families. They had several good reasons for doing so. Increasing land prices in the northern colonies dampened the wanderlust of restless pioneers. Those living on the edge of "civilization" and the Indian lands faced growing hostilities between Indians and European settlers. Increasing tensions also loomed between English settlers and the Germans and Scots-Irish in Pennsylvania. For a growing number of Pennsylvania Quakers, the increasing role of politics in the lives of some Friends, coupled with ever more lavish displays of wealth, led many Friends of the northern colonies to consider moving farther into the backcountry.

Pioneers chose to make the arduous and often risky trip along what is called the "Great Wagon Road," also known as the Philadelphia Wagon Road, its point of origin. (So many Quakers traveled down this route that some called it the Quaker Road.) The name is misleading for two reasons. First, it was initially only one wagon trail in Pennsylvania in the 1720s. From there, it inched into Maryland. By the mid-century, it had reached the Virginia towns of Staunton, Winchester and Martinsburg. Soon it ambled through Roanoke, and by 1760, it had reached as far south as the Moravian village in modern-day Winston-Salem and even Salisbury. Smaller branches snaked outward in all directions. Another section came through what is now Vance County and coursed into Granville County, then through Durham County and eventually into Orange County, where Snow Camp was founded.

Second, the "roads" at that time were no more than footpaths, initially walked by Indians and then white traders, explorers and settlers. As the traffic from the north increased, trading paths once the width of a horse soon widened into roads that could accommodate large wagons.

Soon the backcountry that surrounded Snow Camp swarmed with settlers. By 1767, there were thirteen thousand whites and seven hundred slaves in Orange County. Most were yeoman farmers who settled on "plantations," tracts of land from one hundred to five hundred acres.

The husbands and fathers from Pennsylvania, Maryland and Virginia left their families and headed southward to scout lands in the Piedmont around Cane Creek. Arriving in the fall, they set up temporary quarters—usually pole shacks or log cabins—and then cleared small patches of land for gardens. They often used local hunters, known as guides, to lead them to their new lands.

There are three other spellings of Cane Creek: Cain Creek, Cains Creek and Kane Creek. In the 1770 map by John Collet, it is spelled Cain Creek. In one oral tradition, it was spelled Kane Creek, probably named after the earliest settler, William Kane. Still another tradition is that it was called Cane Creek because the early settlers found sugar cane growing there. Writing in the May 12, 1912 issue of the *Siler City Messenger*, however, Josh U. Way points out that he had fished all up and down Cane Creek and had never seen any cane growing there. Interestingly, there used to be a fall Molasses Festival held at the Snow Camp Outdoor Theatre, where molasses was made from local sugar cane.

Having staked their claims, the settlers returned home but then set out for their new lands the next spring. They covered maybe ten miles a day on the winding paths and dusty narrow roads. Usually a few families moved in small groups together and then settled within several miles of each other. The larger region itself was settled by Scots-Irish and Germans from Pennsylvania. Indeed, Herman Husband called the area "second Pennsylvania." Snow Camp was settled in the 1740s, and many of the initial residents were Quakers. Some of the best records available are from Cane Creek Friends Meeting. The Friends arrived in Snow Camp as early as 1749. The Chamness, Pike, Brown and Wright families bore children here in 1749. Other family names included Wells, Laughlin, Martin, Aldrage, Jones, Kemp, Carter and Tidwell.

The same was the case for Spring Friends Meeting. The families of Henry Holliday, Thomas Lindley and Hugh Laughlin scouted the lands in the fall of 1750. They left the area and headed back up north to Pennsylvania, where they loaded up their families into wagons and moved south to their new home in 1751. Along the dirty route, trees sometimes had to be felled to make room for the wide wagons. The heavy wagons often bogged down in muddy trails or stirred up clouds of choking dust. Sometimes goods and wares were tossed aside to lighten the load for the straining oxen that pulled the loaded wagons. If you were lucky, you might find a home to stay in at night; if not, then you were at the mercy of God and the whims of wild animals, torrential rains or other natural worries.

But the arduous journey that took several months was worth the effort. Land had become expensive in the North, especially in Pennsylvania. In North Carolina, it was often one-tenth the price of land in Pennsylvania. And the joy of freedom and adventure was once again available to the settlers.

Ownership of the land was difficult to document and was often not settled until later in the eighteenth century. The reasons are complicated and beyond the scope of this work, but a concise summary of the problem provides some illumination. John Carteret, Earl Granville, was granted one-eighth of the North Carolina land in 1744 by King George II. As was typical for his day, he hired others to manage the lands for him. In his absence, however, unscrupulous men took charge of selling the land. They might "sell" land, but in many instances, they did not record the transaction. Sometimes the same tract of land was sold to several people. Thus, there was considerable confusion among landholders and eventually hostility between settlers and those who owned rights to their land.

At that time, Snow Camp was in what was Bladen and Anson Counties. In 1752, Orange County was formed, and Snow Camp was officially part of this county. When Chatham County was lined off in 1771, its boundary was just a few miles south of Snow Camp. As one can imagine, keeping track of legal records was difficult. For large families, maintaining birth records was confusing because the county of birth was often perplexing. An older child may have been born in Orange County, but the younger siblings may have been born in Chatham County, even though the house never moved. As the decades went by, it became even more complex. Alamance County, home of present-day Snow Camp, was divided off from Orange County in 1849. In 1895, the Chatham County line was redrawn. As Bobbie Teague quips in her history of Cane Creek Friends Meeting, the meetinghouse has been in Anson, Bladen, Orange, Chatham and Alamance Counties without ever moving!

The legendary story of Simon Dixon is well documented and reveals much about the early settlement. This hardy entrepreneur hailed from Lancaster, Pennsylvania. According to one story, in the spring and summer of 1749 (though the dates vary according to the sources), he surveyed a piece of land off Cane (Cain) Creek, where he built a small cabin and cleared enough land to produce a year's yield of corn for a simple homestead. Lonely and depressed, he left for home but returned to settle with his wife, Elizabeth Allen Dixon; his mother and stepfather; and two sisters, Rebecca and Ruth. He brought with him two millstones, and after settling his family down and building a rock house, he began work on his mill. For years, this mill served Snow Camp until it was shut down in the early 1900s. The foundation stones for the mill can still be seen today, as well as a long stone wall he built that lines Sylvan Road as it rises from Cane Creek to Cane Creek Quaker Meeting.

Others arrived at the same time or shortly after. The new settlers' names are still around today: Allen, Stout, Thompson, McPherson, Pike, Holladay, Zachary, Woody, Newlin, Carter, Braxton and Hadley, to name a few. Soon, their small corn and wheat farms were quite productive, so there arose the need for specialization. Just a few miles to the east, Lindley's Mill was constructed, and while it has changed hands and buildings through the decades, it is still in operation today. A quick drive around Snow Camp today takes you by several roads named "— Mill." The number of mills in this small area demonstrates just how many farmers were there and how fertile the land was. But farmers needed more than mills. Women needed sewing supplies and pots. Children needed shoes. So stores sprang up. John Allen ran a store from his house, and his wife, Rachel Allen, administered natural medicines.

THE JOHN ALLEN HOUSE
AND THE RANDOLPH COBLE HOUSE

In the mid- to late 1700s, settlers in the Piedmont of North Carolina lived in a variety of shelters, and economic class determined the style and size of the dwelling. Farmers, husbandmen and yeomen were prevalent, as well as numerous poor settlers. Small farmers generally lived in one- or two-room log houses or frame buildings. On the back, a lean-to might have been attached. A large fireplace was used for cooking and heat. Amenities were few: beds with corn shuck, straw or feather mattresses; stools; benches; and maybe a chest of drawers. The poorest lived in what could only be called shacks with dirt floors. With this information, we can look at the house occupied by the Allen family around 1780.

In 1751, John Allen II came to Cane Creek from Chester County, Pennsylvania, procured the land from Lord Granville and then returned home. In 1754, John Allen II died, but his son John III and family returned to Snow Camp.

John Allen III married Rachel Stout, and the two built a small cabin on six hundred acres of land that he inherited from his father. A few years later, he built a larger cabin. He chose oak and ash logs for his new house. The building had two floors, a cellar, a front and back porch and a small room on the back. Typical of his day, he cut notches in the shape of a V for the corner joints in the hand-hewn logs.

Logs used in houses were not squared, so there were gaps between the timbers. These spaces were filled with daubing, a mixture of clay and straw. Originally, there were no windows. There may have been two reasons for this.

John Allen House. *Courtesy of the North Carolina Department of Cultural Resources, Alamance Battleground State Historic Site.*

One, glass was taxed, so the Allens may have chosen to leave them out for economic purposes. But windows were not airtight; thus, cold air could seep through in the winter, which may have been another reason for their omission.

Since most families in the area had small one-room houses with dirt floors, the two-story structure complete with cellar indicates that the Allens were of some means. The size of the house may have been for practical reasons as well: John and his wife, Rachel, had twelve children. Still, other families had numerous children, so again, the Allen house suggests that the family was "rich."

Quakers in other states, such as Pennsylvania, were shrewd businesspeople. When they migrated to North Carolina, they brought their business prowess with them, so some degree of wealth was quite common among the North Carolina Piedmont Quakers. Based on the size of the house and the contents, John, Rachel and their children enjoyed luxuries that those of lesser means did not have.

The first floor served as a kitchen and dining room, as well as a living room and bedroom. Families typically lived in front of the large fireplace, which provided heat in the winter and light throughout the year. Most of the family activity centered on the fireplace. The children and Rachel were in charge of maintaining the fire.

Meals were prepared in the large, open-hearth fireplace. Big iron cooking pots, such as Dutch ovens and skillets, were used to prepare meals. Pot hangers, called trammels or swinging cranes, allowed the pots to be swung close to or away from the fire.

How did the Allens light their house without windows? Doors were opened in the warm seasons, and in the evenings, candles that were either hand-dipped or molded from beeswax and tallow burned until bedtime. Since neither kerosene nor oil was yet available, Betty lamps and reed/rush lights (which used fish oil or grease) were used.

The family walked up a spiral stairway to go to bed for the night. Interestingly, while other cabins in the area had open lofts for the sleeping quarters, the upstairs of the Allen House was closed off from the downstairs. The placement of the fireplace deserves mention. It was in the room, not on the outside of the building. Only the chimney could be seen outside. This upped the risk of fire (the reason most people did not construct the fireplace inside the building), but it heated the room more efficiently.

John Allen was a man who wore many hats. He was a farmer, teacher, craftsman and even lawyer. He ran a small store from his house, and the room in the back of the building might have been used for this purpose. Items sold would have included materials and implements for sewing: bolts of cloth, thimbles, needles, buttons and buttonmolds and knitting needles. Other items probably included pots, pencils and even ladies' shoes. We know that Rachel was an itinerant doctor. She went door to door with her herbal items and recipes. At home, she ran what today would be called a pharmacy. Arsenic, mercury, calomel, patent medicines and spices lined the shelves.

Beulah Oyama Allen recorded one of Rachel's recipes for a burn: "To make ointment to cure a Burn or Scald take the tops of high Rattlesnake [a plant] in the Spring of the year and fresh may Butter and pound them well together then make it up in Balls let it lie about Six weeks then put it in a Kettle over the fire let them Simmer Well then Strain them out keep it for use."

The John Allen House was moved to the Alamance Battleground State Historic Site in 1967 and then restored. Many of the original possessions were kept in the family and date back to the late 1700s and early 1800s. A

Chippendale desk and Chippendale six-drawer chest are probably the most notable. Other items include a tilt-top candle stand, a case clock and a maple ladder-back chair.

If we could go back in time to visit the Allens and other families, we would find several familiar tools and items, as well as a host of odd implements. Many upper-class families owned looms. Beds had ropes, not springs, to hold up the sleepy occupants, and trundle beds (smaller beds that slid out from under the larger beds) allowed maximum use of space.

The following items in the exhibit of the Allen House at the Battleground provide a glimpse of the numerous chores a family performed throughout the year: flax wheel, kraut cutter and barrel, two-man crosscut saw, T-handled augers (to drill holes), drawknife (to shape wooden handles), shaving horse (bench-like vise), broad axe, froe (used to make shingles), planes, large chisel, compass, pot handles, leather mold and leather vise.

There were no trimmed grass lawns in those days. Clean, swept dirt yards kept fires from reaching the buildings, and rodents and snakes, which preferred foliage rather than dirt, were kept at bay.

The original Allen house did not have a smokehouse. This was added in 1825. Smokehouses were used to cure and preserve meat. Animals were

Interior of the John Allen House. *Courtesy of the North Carolina Department of Cultural Resources, Alamance Battleground State Historic Site.*

slaughtered in the winter to prevent spoilage, and the meat was cut into smaller quarters, which were cured or smoked. Seasonings, such as salt or sugar, pepper and even molasses, were applied to the meat, which was then hung over a fire of hickory chips and cured for several days. Smaller portions of meats could also be cured by placing them in alternating layers of salt in barrels for several weeks.

Descendants of the Allen family occupied the house from the 1800s until 1929. During this time, several improvements were made to the original log structure. Around 1900, many families in North Carolina grew tired of their primitive log houses. In order to look wealthier, families covered their log houses with clapboard siding. The Allen family was no exception. They added two glass windows to the front of the building and then nailed clapboards on the two ends of the house.

One example of this renovation can be seen in the picture of the Randolph Coble House on the following page. The original two-story structure, unlike the Allen House, still remains in Snow Camp, but it is not in its original location. It is not clear when the Randolph Coble House was built. One source places it around 1750–80 based on its Swiss-Palatine style. This could certainly be true because that style was present in Pennsylvania Dutch communities, and many of the initial settlers of Snow Camp hailed from Pennsylvania. Also, the style was employed by nearby Moravians. However, birth dates and other records do not support this. It is more probable that the log house was built in the mid-1800s by Randolph Coble, who ran a mercantile store nearby beginning in 1850. Just like the Allen House, clapboards were put on the sides to modernize the building.

Joe Coble removed the clapboards in the 1960s. People from the area rented the building, and rumor has it that parties were held there as well. Eventually, the house was purchased by Augustin Maissen, who was a professor at University of North Carolina–Chapel Hill. Dr. Maissen had to return to Switzerland because of declining health, so the house—along with the contents, which included numerous antiques—as well as land, was put up for auction. The price of the house was deemed prohibitive by many. But a fire actually led to the purchase of the house by Buddy and Nancy Aldridge in 1989. Because of the fire and smoke damage, as well as destruction of the plumbing and electrical cords, the price was dropped dramatically. After purchasing it, the Aldridges renovated it every weekend until they moved into it in 1995. Still, if you look around carefully you can see some of the black coloring on the oak logs that remains from the fire

Randolph Coble House, early 1900s. *Courtesy of Nancy and Buddy Aldridge.*

A walk around the house takes one back to yesterday. V-notch logs are filled with a substance that looks like the old mud daubing used by pioneers. The ceiling height in the original part is lower than houses today. The present house also has an added-on kitchen. When the Aldridges pulled off the old tongue-and-groove wallboards for more renovation, they found the old wattle-and-daub chinking still in between the exterior logs. Even today, many older residents can claim they were born in "the old log cabin over there."

CANE CREEK FRIENDS QUAKER MEETING

The Piedmont of North Carolina has a rich tradition of church history. By the 1750s, several Protestant denominations were in existence in Alamance County. A congregation of Scots-Irish Presbyterians had been meeting in the Haw Fields area, about eighteen miles northeast of Snow Camp, possibly as early as 1750. About fifteen miles south of Snow Camp, a fiery preacher from Massachusetts, Shubal Stearns, settled down and soon began Sandy Creek Separate Baptist Church in 1755. By 1757, the membership was somewhere between six hundred and nine hundred people (the numbers vary according to scholars). Roughly to the west, Germans took up residence, bringing with them their own brand of Protestantism. The historic and renovated original Brick Reformed Church building still stands today, and special services are held there. The building is over 250 years old.

From the very beginning, however, Snow Camp's early history has been determined by Quakers. Old maps show the "Meeting House." Many of the initial Snow Camp settlers were Quakers, and as the decades went by, if you weren't Quaker, you or someone in your family probably married one. Today, the standard joke around Snow Camp is that all the locals are cousins, in one way or another, dating from way back when.

Who are the Quakers? In the 1640s and '50s, there was a restless spirit moving among simple folk in the British Isles. Its founder was Puritan George Fox, who was born in Leicestershire, England, in 1624. He developed the Quaker belief in the Light of Christ that lived within all. Rather than being dependent on the Bible or a priest or minister, Quakers could receive revelations directly from God. Women were seen as equals with men. Worship was silent; dress was plain. Some Quakers were overcome with "shaking" when they received revelations, thus the name of Quakers.

The controversial theology did not sit well with the established denominations. Persecutions followed, and some fled to the new colonies across the Atlantic to escape persecution, only to find it again—this time, from the Puritans in New England. Soon Quaker William Penn received a grant in 1681 to found a colony that he organized around Quaker ideals. By 1683, over three thousand Friends had begun new lives in the Quaker-friendly colony.

Quakers also found a home in southeastern Virginia around 1660. The new land proved inhospitable to Friends, but there was indeed Light to the south. As required in its charter, North Carolina was open to all religions, so Quakers moved to the northeastern portion of North Carolina in the area now known as Perquimans. Soon, there was a thriving community of Friends.

Following Quaker tradition, in 1750, the group that was to become Cane Creek Meeting sought sponsorship by the Yearly Meeting of Perquimans County. There was no immediate response, but Abigail Pike and Rachel Wright, along with others, trekked two hundred miles east to Perquimans Meeting to request that Cane Creek Meeting be officially recognized. On August 31, 1751, the Friends at Cane Creek were given monthly meeting status.

Abigail Pike deserves more attention. She was a Friends minister, and she often traveled to Quaker meetings. Tradition notes that this spunky woman spoke in army camps during the American Revolution, perhaps visiting both the English and American camps.

With official recognition, the Cane Creek Friends, who had been meeting in homes, could now construct a meetinghouse. Like other places of worship, a small structure was built of logs on land owned by John Stanfield. In 1764, land and a house were donated to the meeting by William and Rebecca Marshall. The house may have been used as a new place of worship or else the Friends built a new meeting place at this location. The meeting prospered, and a third meetinghouse was constructed sometime in the early 1800s. It was destroyed by fire in 1879, but a new building was completed a year later.

What was worship like in the old days at Cane Creek? Before the first log meetinghouse was built, Quakers met in their homes, sometimes with other

Above: Tradition says that this was the first meetinghouse of Cane Creek Friends Meeting. *Courtesy of Snow Camp Historical Society.*

Below: The 1880 building of Cane Creek Friends Meeting. *Courtesy of Cane Creek Friends Meeting Historical Room.*

families or sometimes only with their immediate family. The participants observed times of silence. Once the meetinghouse was built, two times of worship were observed by the community: First Day (Sunday) and Fifth Day (Thursday). Quakers originally did not use the regular names of days because they were named after gods. For example, Thursday was Thor's Day. To use this designation implied that one acknowledged other gods and honored them with special days. Thus, Quakers simply used First Day, Second Day, etc.

Friends in simple dress, including hats and bonnets, would arrive and assemble in the room. The leader of the meeting was called a recorded minister. A recorded minister had the gift of ministry, which meant a special wisdom and talent for speaking in meetings. Because of this, he or she sat at the front of the room and faced the rows of men and women who typically sat on benches on separate sides of the unheated room. The Friends remained silent until the Light inspired them to speak. When inspired, they stood, removed their hats or bonnets and spoke about what had been revealed to themselves. Some meetings experienced silence for the entire time. When the recorded minister believed enough time had passed, the meeting was adjourned.

It is probable that Cane Creek Friends Meeting retained this form of "open worship" until the late 1800s, when a nationwide revival blazed its way into the Tarheel State. When Thomas C. Hodgin preached a revival at Cane Creek in the late 1800s, he challenged the meeting to hire a pastor who could better serve them. In 1909, Cane Creek began a new era in its storied life when pastors Miles and Georgia Reece were hired part time. Georgia taught at Sylvan School, as did many later pastors at Cane Creek. In 1941, Elbert Newlin, who had served at Cane Creek while a student at Guilford College in Greensboro, was hired as the first full-time pastor for $100 a month plus house rent.

Once the new mode of ministry and worship changed, so did other aspects of the meeting. Music was most likely introduced into the service at this time. A small, portable organ was used initially, but in 1915, Hayes Thompson donated a large reed organ to the meeting. In 1920, Callie Green spearheaded fundraising to purchase a piano. One unique innovation was an electrical system. While electric lines did not run through Snow Camp at this time, a thirty-two-volt battery was purchased and the building wired for just over $155. In 1935, "power" came to the area, and the battery system was no longer needed.

During the First World War, Cane Creek, along with other local Quaker meetings, began a mission for "the special purpose of raising funds for the war victims in Europe." In the ledger book of William P. Stout, there are notations from mid-1917 to mid-1919 for collections received from Cane Creek, Plainfield, South Fork, Providence, Centre, Rocky River, Saxapahaw and Woody's Grove Meetings. The records show that over $650 was raised.

Revivals were held in Cane Creek Meeting in the early 1900s. This was a huge shift from the normally staid Quaker practice of silent worship. Preaching was "good," according to Cane Creek Friend Kyle Kimball. He recalls that three women preached at some of the revivals.

Tragedy struck on January 4, 1942. Members arrived on that Sunday and watched in dismay as their building burned to the ground. All was lost except for the piano and a few chairs. A prayer service was held later that day, and a building committee meeting was set up for that evening in Sylvan School. The basement for the new building was dug using teams of horses and mules supplied by Dolph Whitehead, Odie Stuart, Will Kimball, Kyle Kimball and P.H. Stephens. Kyle Kimball harnessed up his plow to a team of horses and dug up the ground. A large plate was then hooked up to two other horses and pulled to scrape the dirt out. Then the process was repeated until the hole was deep enough for the basement. Nathan Wright set up a sawmill near the site, and locals brought logs to be cut for lumber. Lannie Thompson and Charlie Stout were two of the carpenters. Nine months later, donations from all over the North Carolina Yearly Meeting, as well as from other churches and individuals and the collective labors of locals, were manifest in a new brick building. Dedicated on October 6 of that same year, it still stands today. Several additions have since followed through the years: a front porch and steps, a pastor's study and kitchen, a handicapped ramp and, in 1980, a fellowship hall.

Today, Cane Creek remains involved in the North Carolina Yearly Meeting. When the Yearly Meeting held a recent centennial gathering, Cane Creek members displayed various historical items from their collection. The youth group often goes to Quaker Lake Camp. Some men have recently become involved in disaster relief after storms. The meeting supports the Sword of Peace Outdoor Theatre with a special day for the actors complete with a meal. The men's meeting is quite active, and they have a monthly breakfast. A Fall Festival fundraiser features breakfast biscuits, hot dogs for lunch and then Brunswick stew (from the recipe of Cleo Griffin) for the evening meal. Crafts are also for sale at the event. Young people meet on Sunday evenings, and Cane Creek Meeting also joins together with Rocky River Friends Meeting for youth meetings.

On Saturday, October 6, 2001, Cane Creek Friends Meeting celebrated its 250th year with a two-day affair. Saturday featured a genealogy workshop. On Sunday, Lesa McPherson, John Porter, Monroe McVey, Larry Griffin, Marilyn Matthews, Bobbie Teague and John Allen led the service. Dr. Jay Marshall, dean of Earlham School of Religion, gave the sesquibicentennial message. Those in attendance enjoyed Sunday morning worship and then lunch. In the afternoon, the Abigail Pike historical marker was unveiled. Representatives from the North Carolina Yearly Meeting and past members were part of the 250 to 300 people attending the celebration. Former governor Bob Scott, Congressman Howard Coble and other politicians attended as well. A time capsule was put together to be opened in 2051.

A lot has changed since 1751, and Cane Creek Friends Meeting has met those changes through persistence and guidance by the Light. Today, the meeting continues its legacy as one of the mainstays of the Snow Camp community.

SPRING FRIENDS QUAKER MEETING

Thanks to Algie Newlin's book *Friends "at the Spring,"* the history of Spring Friends Meeting is much more extensive than that of Cane Creek Meeting or any other religious denomination in Snow Camp. Newlin was born and raised in Snow Camp and was professor of history at Guilford College in Greensboro for forty-two years. A lot can be learned about the history of Snow Camp in the story of Spring Meeting.

Quakers from miles around rode wagons and horses and walked on foot on First Days and Fifth Days to meet together at Cane Creek Friends Meeting. But as the population grew, some Friends felt that it was more practical to have a meeting closer to home. According to Quaker policy, Quakers wanting to form a new meeting had to ask permission from a "mother" meeting. Since Cane Creek was the only Quaker meeting in the Piedmont that was receiving new Quaker settlers every year, it soon birthed six Quaker meetings. One of these was Spring Friends Meeting, just nine miles east of Cane Creek Meeting.

The history of Spring Friends Meeting is a tumultuous one. Early pioneers, such as the Hollidays, Lindleys, Laughlins, Braxtons, Woodys, Newlins and Carters, settled in the area east of Cane Creek and formed the core of the meeting. As early as 1761, maybe even the 1750s, a small group of Quakers were gathering by a spring or springs (traditions vary) for worship. The Friends who gathered there wavered in their allegiance to the meeting, as demonstrated in the following story.

Probably sometime in the 1750s, attendance had fallen dramatically. There are several potential reasons for this. If the time of the decline

Spring Friends Meeting building. Built in 1907, the structure was listed in the National Register of Historic Places in 1987. *Courtesy of the author.*

was after 1755, then the lack of interest was no doubt due in part to the influence of the fiery Baptists in the area, who also shared the building with the Friends. About eighteen miles southward, Shubal Stearns, a Separate Baptist preacher and leader of what today is called the Sandy Creek Revival, was lighting up the region with his incendiary sermons and revivals. Possibly the few Quakers who met in the building had cast their lot with their Baptist neighbors. Or maybe apathy, combined with attrition due to death and the departure of others for greener pastures, depleted the membership. There are four versions of what happened to bring the meeting by the spring back to life again. All involve a certain John Carter. The most probable story, according to Algie Newlin's history, was related by John Carter in 1796 when he rode with Thomas Scattergood to a gathering at Spring Meeting. Here is Scattergood's version of the rebirth of the Quakers who assembled at the spring for meetings:

> As our friend John Carter and I rode together, he informed me, that in his younger years, being visited by the day spring from on high [the Light] he sought much to find a place to rest his soul, and joined the Baptists. After a time he grew dissatisfied with their mode of worship, not feeling that peace which he was in pursuit of...At this time the little company of Friends in the neighborhood had grown weak to neglect their meeting, and had given consent for the baptists [sic] to hold meetings in their meetinghouse. For some time his mind was impressed with apprehension, that it was required of him to go and sit down by himself in the meeting-house; but he put it off, being ashamed. At length he went by a private way and sat down alone and was greatly refreshed...One day in going to meeting he met with [a neighbor], who asked him where he was going, and he told him honestly, "I am going to Meeting;"...Next time he went seven of his neighbors on hearing of his going, joined him and in process of time he was united to the Society of Friends; zeal and religion revived among them, and there is now a large meeting called Spring Meeting, which we are at today.

During the Revolutionary War, Spring Meeting played a small part in the few local battles. Some of its members were close kin to Loyalist soldiers involved in that skirmish known as Pyle's Massacre or Pyle's Hacking Match. The Battle of Lindley's Mill literally took place near the front yard of Spring Meeting. Many of the injured from both sides were tended to by Spring Meeting members. (More on these battles to follow.)

In 1793, Spring Meeting requested and was granted full independence from Cane Creek. Spring Friends Monthly Meeting was now on its own.

During this time, several leaders emerged. Zachariah Dicks, a respected Quaker, attended several Quaker meetings, Spring Meeting being one of them, in the Piedmont. In 1803, he traveled to and implored Quakers in Georgia and South Carolina to move west to avoid the troubles of slavery.

He followed his own advice and in 1809 moved to Ohio. Dicks's son-in-law Jonathan Lindley was a member of Spring Meeting. He had a distinguished career as a North Carolina politician. In 1811, he and his family left for Indiana. William Lindley was the clerk of Spring Meeting from 1775 to 1784. With the hard work and encouragement of these and other leaders, Spring Meeting's membership swelled. It had close ties to three other meetings: Eno, Chatham and South Fork.

After the Revolutionary War, Quaker meetings around Snow Camp faced their first tests of loyalty to their denomination. Four foes stood in their way: mammon, slavery, new prospects in the West and new churches of other denominations. Throughout North Carolina, morals and religion were tossed aside after the War of the Revolution. People of all religious stripes forgot their convictions and instead lived lives of sin. For the Friends in local meetings, many members were disowned for a variety of reasons, including babies born out of wedlock, drunkenness, fighting and materialism, as well as deism and general apathy. All denominations were affected by a huge rise in debauchery at this time. The large membership of Spring Meeting slowly dwindled with these disownments.

Slavery was on the rise in the Tarheel State during this time, but the largest population of slaves was in the eastern region. In the Piedmont, farmers in northern Alamance County owned more slaves than those in the southern portion of the county. Quakers objected to slavery, and one form of protest was moving from the area to what was then called the "northwest," what today includes Ohio, Indiana and other portions of that region. As Quaker opposition against slavery grew, so did animosity against Quakers in the Piedmont. Many families left rather than experience persecution, which included having their marriages invalidated and thus their children declared illegitimate.

Moving was painful. The Coble family history provides a glimpse of the preparations for their departure from Randolph County. The long distance west and the rough roads meant furniture was left behind. Instead, only the basics for survival were packed: provisions, utensils and farm implements. The rest of the space in the wagon was for the children and wife. Women made clothes for the journey, while girls made noodles, peeled and dried apples and filled jars with honey. Boys shelled corn for meal. Men prepared the wagons and harnesses for the arduous journey. The wagon had a rifle, a chain, an ax, a hatchet, a shovel, revolvers and ammunition, as well as food. Not all rode in wagons; some walked, others rode on horseback and some herded the livestock along the way.

Third, the lure of land, both to settle and speculate, beckoned Quakers and others westward, initially to Georgia and South Carolina, then to Tennessee and eventually to Ohio and Indiana. It is probable that most families, filled with "frontier fever," took the long wagon ride to greener pastures because of the prospects of enterprise. Families of long-standing Spring Meeting members, like the Andrews, Lindleys, Newlins, Hollidays, Carters and Woodys, left in droves. Families of other faiths moved west as well. The migrations did not affect Spring Meeting until the early to mid-1800s. In 1811, Spring Meeting member Jonathon Lindley led a wagon train of approximately two hundred people from Snow Camp, some of them from Spring Meeting, to the southern region of Indiana. One story recalls that Ann Long Hadley rode her mare Skip all the way to Indiana, a trip of nine hundred miles.

Many Spring Meeting members attended revivals in Baptist, Methodist and Christian churches in the area. Locally, Presbyterian James McGready started the fires of conversion in the Piedmont around 1791. Those who attended saw the converted falling to the ground, shouting and crying. The first "camp meeting" took place in Hawfields, just eighteen miles northeast of Snow Camp, in late 1801. Revival soon spread across the recalcitrantly irreligious Tarheel State, especially westward. It lasted until 1803, but interdenominational camp meetings were held sporadically through 1809. Fiery preaching, a focus on individualism and exuberant singing—none of which were part of Quaker worship and polity—were powerful draws for the sinful and backslidden. While interdenominational unity was initially the goal, soon theological differences led to denominational feuds. By the 1830s, many Spring Meeting members joined the Methodist denomination.

In the early 1800s, Quaker meetings began hosting local subscription schools. As early as 1818, Spring Meeting sponsored its first school. In 1835, Spring Meeting began its first First Day School, as did Chatham, Eno and Southfork Meetings, all of which were associated with Spring Meeting.

For Quaker meetings in the Piedmont, an increasingly strict piety also contributed to the decline. The Hicksite-Orthodox theological split that echoed other denominational theological divisions of this time led to further losses. Coupled with the increasingly sympathetic support of abolition, the damage had been done, and Spring Meeting was a part of the fallout.

By the time of the Civil War, Spring Friends Meeting had lost nearly all of its members. In December 1854, one traveler attended an appointed service at Spring Meeting that was attended by sixty to seventy people, nearly all of whom were not Spring Meeting members. On many First Days, only three or four Spring Meeting members were in attendance. The meetinghouse was in terrible disrepair.

The Civil War did not help. The few male members of Spring Meeting were conscripted by the Confederate army. Driven by Southern patriotism, some young Quaker men joined the ranks. After the war, many Quakers in the Snow Camp area were subjected to abuse by their Confederate neighbors. Confederate money was worthless, so Spring Meeting members were reduced to poverty. Aware of the situation, the Baltimore Association set up missions for the beleaguered South, and Snow Camp was the recipient of this benevolence. But as the years went by, mills and new farming techniques led to an economic recovery for all. As conditions improved, Spring Meeting membership swelled.

Part of this increase was because the Quakers nationally initiated and experienced a revival. As they did so, the Quakers adopted many of the practices of their Protestant neighbors. Exuberant singing, powerful preaching from a pulpit and more emphasis on the Bible were now evident. Revivals were the new medium for salvation, and Spring Meeting, like other churches in the area, held revivals from the 1870s to the 1950s. Evangelism was in the air. Sunday school was formed, and home altars were built. As membership grew, the aging meetinghouse was replaced in either 1876 or '77. Ellen and Martha Woody became missionaries and ministered in Cuba. A new meetinghouse was constructed in 1907, and it still stands today. Spring Meeting, like many other Quaker meetings, hired a pastor to serve its members.

World Wars I and II challenged the Spring Meeting membership. Hannah Marlet's son was killed in the First World War, and Perisho McBane was killed in a gas attack. Many Spring Meeting members signed cards of protest that were sent to the World Peace Foundation in 1935. Hal Hargrove was enlisted, but he drove a truck for the army. Still, local Quaker conscientious objectors in Snow Camp and their families were the victims of much criticism, and even today, descendants of these families will not discuss the matter. Quaker resistance to the wars led to the decline in membership in Spring Meeting.

In 1970, members of Spring Meeting began planning for the 200th anniversary celebration. The Alamance County Historical Association announced that it would install a roadside marker to commemorate Spring Meeting. On Saturday, October 13, 1973, the celebration began and continued into Sunday. Spring Meeting also supported the community in the 1970s. It hosted a local Girl Scout troop and donated funds for the

Sword of Peace Outdoor Theatre. Christmas programs and hymn singings were enjoyed by all.

Spring Meeting experienced yet another decline in membership as the century neared its end. Disputes over traditional Quaker worship versus the more evangelical style erupted. In the first few years of the twenty-first century, attendance had dwindled to almost no one.

But today, Spring Friends Meeting is back on its feet. Attendance is increasing, and the more traditional style of quiet worship is now the centerpiece of its spiritual life.

THE AMERICAN REVOLUTION

Snow Camp was involved one way or another in four important incidents in the history of the Revolutionary War in North Carolina. The first, the Regulators Revolt, has been called by some the first defiant act against the British in the colonies. It was actually a protest waged in 1771 against unfair taxation by unscrupulous, greedy representatives of the Crown in the Piedmont of the Tarheel State. The protest turned bloody as both sides squared off several miles north of Snow Camp. But the instigator of the protest was Herman Husband, a Quaker who was originally a member of Cane Creek Friends Meeting.

Ten years later, three events took place. First, Dr. John Pyle of Snow Camp led a small contingent of Loyalist soldiers in a skirmish with Patriots northwest of the area. Second, General Cornwallis marched his tired army south after his "victory" in the Battle of Guilford Courthouse, which took place in modern-day Greensboro. While he indeed did win, it was more a Pyrrhic victory: he lost many troops, and many more were wounded. As he marched back to Fayetteville, soldiers encamped in the territory around Snow Camp, specifically Dixon's Mill.

Last, there was the Battle of Lindley's Mill, which took place seven miles west of Snow Camp. The battle, which occurred in 1781, has also been called the Battle of Snow Camp.

Herman Husband and the Regulator Movement

In order for the new settlers to document land sales, deeds were drawn. Fees were charged for these transactions, and herein lay a problem. Those who collected the fees and performed the legal transactions ignored the set fees and instead charged what they wanted. The settlers complained, and proper measures were taken in an attempt to ensure that these abuses did not occur again. But still the practice continued. As the years moved along and the fees continued, tensions increased between the landowners and the officials.

A second problem arose as well. If a person could not pay his taxes, then these corrupt officials would use deputies to "distrain" the necessary fees. Property was confiscated if the taxes were not paid. The very tools the settler would use to earn the money to pay his taxes were often distrained. These items were then resold by the officials at a high profit.

Who commanded these "courthouse rings"? The justice of the peace was in control. He chose the jurors for legal cases, and he also selected the deputies who collected the taxes. Higher fees, bribery and favoritism ruled the day for officials who stooped to any level to increase their incomes. All were in some way connected to the gentry powers in the eastern half of North Carolina who refused to relinquish their dominance of the governance of the state. The major ringleader for the residents of Snow Camp was the arrogant, unscrupulous lawyer, merchant, Crown prosecutor and register of deeds, Edmund Fanning. And as he rose in unpopularity, a group of men who would call themselves the Regulators organized in 1766. The Sandy Creek Association was formed to address the rising grievances of the residents. The goal: to elect grass-roots people from its ranks to represent them and their cause in the legislature. Their ringleader: Herman Husband.

Herman Husband (sometimes called Herman Husbands or Harmon Husbands) hailed from Maryland and was a prolific reader and writer. Born an Anglican, he converted to the Presbyterian faith at the age of sixteen and then later joined the Quakers. He was a businessman and speculator in the Piedmont, and while his dealings were specifically with the Separate Baptists who settled south of Snow Camp, he joined Cane Creek Friends Meeting in 1755. His Quaker theology coupled with democratic ideals soon jelled into the political agenda that would unite disparate farmers into a force called the Regulator Movement.

As he dealt with prospective landowners, he became convinced that the corrupt antics of Fanning and his cronies were keeping settlers from buying land (which affected his income). Curbing the corruption, he believed,

Each year around May 16, the Regulator war is reenacted at the Alamance Battleground State Historic Site. *Courtesy of the North Carolina Department of Cultural Resources, Alamance Battleground State Historic Site.*

would increase sales. Since many of his customers were also Separate Baptists, he was closely connected with the meteoric rise of members who needed land. These new landowners quickly became disgruntled settlers who were tired of the mistreatment by Fanning and his ring of tax thugs. Loss of sales, a high regard for religion, democratic principles: all of these factors soon came to a boil. Herman Husband became the de facto leader of the Regulators. Who were his supporters? The answer goes back to Cane Creek Friends Meeting.

Cane Creek Meeting found itself in a controversy in late 1760 and early 1761 over the sexual relationship of Charity Wright and Jehu Stuart. Both Jehu and Charity were disowned by the meeting, leading to divisions in the meeting. The leader of the anti-Wright faction was Herman Husband, who was disowned for his behavior in the meeting. Bobbie Teague, in her history of Cane Creek Friends Meeting, recalls that he took off his shoes, shook the "dirt of Quakerism" off of them, put his shoes back on his feet and then walked away from the meeting, just as Jesus had commanded his disciples to do if they were ever barred from entering a town. His followers in the meeting became part of the cast of the Regulators.

The tactics of the Regulators were confrontational yet within the limits of public civil politics. They organized to present their grievances at advertised meetings where local officials were invited to attend. But they also appeared at court meetings to forcefully retake items that were unscrupulously distrained by local officials. One problem arose, however. The Regulators were divided by a religious line: should they remain pacifist and nonviolent (a typical Quaker and Separate Baptist belief), or should they push further and forcefully persuade the government officials that they meant business? The more frustrated they became, the more blurred the demarcation.

In April 1768, some Regulators went to the Hillsborough courthouse and physically seized a horse that had been distrained for unpaid taxes. Shots were then fired at Fanning's house. Fanning, who was also in charge of the militia, organized his troops immediately, but nothing more came of the matter. However, the stage had been set and the cast of characters was in place. Governor Tryon was made aware of Fanning's abuse of his privileges. Fanning arrested Husband and William Butler on charges of rebellion, which gave the Regulators a real cause: two of their own were being held by the law. A cautious mob of Regulators, the number of whom varies tremendously according to the sources, surrounded Hillsborough as though it was about to attack. Fanning somehow persuaded the angry men to disperse, but the damage had been done. The governor admonished all officials to follow the limits of tax collection as prescribed by law, but the Regulators wanted more. Fanning had to go.

Governor Tryon was rightly worried that more skirmishes would ensue. Colonel Fanning now had an archenemy in the person of Herman Husband. Both officials worried that Husband would lead insurrections in the Piedmont. The trial set for September 1768 was critical for all concerned. What would happen to Husband or the cause of the Regulators? Husband was acquitted, but now, instead of a record, he had a reputation.

By July 1769, several Regulators and sympathizers were elected to represent five counties. The small gains did not outnumber the traditional voices in the Assembly. After the court session in Hillsborough in March 1770, where Fanning and his cronies withstood major legal onslaughts from Regulators, the embarrassments only fueled more opposition. Governor Tryon now believed that the Piedmont, which included Snow Camp, was full of insurrectionists.

In January 1771, the Johnston Riot Act was passed. For one year, retroactive to March 1770, any person who instigated a riot was considered a felon.

Those who resisted arrest or fled were considered outlaws. The law, which breached statutory and common law, was clearly meant for the Regulators and, more specifically, those who had participated in the Hillsborough riot in September 1770. In the meantime, Husband was eventually incarcerated in Newborn, far to the east of Orange County and the Regulators. A grand jury refused to indict him, and he was released. The fear of an assault on the prison by 2,200 mobilized and angry Regulators may have had something to do with his release as well.

Backed by the Johnston Riot Act, Tryon called out the eastern militia, a force of around eight hundred men, and set a course west, hoping to add more militia as he marched toward the Piedmont. This proved to be difficult: while loyal to the Crown, many of the local militia members were sympathetic to the Regulator cause. Still, about 270 additional soldiers joined the ranks. By May 16, Tryon's army was positioned at the battle site a few miles south of today's Burlington to face a small army of Regulators. Noticeably absent was Herman Husband. Was he still loyal to his Quaker pacifist beliefs? More likely, his fear of being captured as an insurrectionist may have had more to do with his absence.

Why this band of Regulators assembled before Tryon's formidable force is not clear. Many in the area did not want any battle at all. Some think that the intent was to present Tryon with enough force to convince him to retreat. Even Tryon wanted to avoid any conflict at all.

On May 15, the Regulators sent messengers to work out a reasonable solution to the impending conflict. The next morning, Tryon, clearly affronted at the audacity of these rioters to demand his compliance to their demands, read the Regulators the Riot Act, a practice that had originated in England decades prior to the Johnston Riot Act (thus the phrase "read them the riot act"). As per the act, they had one hour to respond.

In order to delay the onslaught, the Regulators asked for an exchange of prisoners or even a compromise. In a last-ditch effort to avoid conflict, the influential Presbyterian minister Reverend David Caldwell intervened, hoping to mediate a settlement. The Regulators were advised by the minister to go home unless charges were pending against them. These should instead surrender. Just as Caldwell moved out of the line of fire, Tryon called for the first volley.

Confusion surrounds what happened next, but the bottom line is that the battle itself lasted about two hours. As victory became inevitable, Tryon called for a truce, and the dead were quickly buried. Tryon offered pardons to the Regulators, and according to his report, around three thousand surrendered their arms and took an oath to serve the present government, not the insurrection of the Regulators.

But the war was not over.

Tryon, along with General Waddell, set out to terrorize the homes and farms of Regulators along Cane Creek, Richland Creek and Sandy Creek. He ruined their crops, burned their houses, stole livestock and took flour from local mills to feed his militia. Since the Quakers and Separate Baptists were sympathetic to the Regulator cause, he targeted them especially. Tryon deliberately settled in the Sandy Creek area for a week. On May 21, he destroyed Herman Husband's six-hundred-acre plantation, including all of the crops, fences and the house. In Snow Camp, six wagonloads of flour were confiscated, and miller Simon Dixon was forced to give up three more wagons filled with barrels of flour.

On June 9, Tryon put out bounties, dead or alive, for Herman Husband, James Hunter, Rednap Howell and William Butner. The prize? One hundred pounds and one thousand acres of land. None of the men were captured. Fourteen prisoners were seized and then tried in Hillsborough on June 15. Twelve were convicted, but only six were hanged; the others were pardoned. Tryon and Edmund Fanning then fled to New York for new political opportunities, leaving a badly divided colony behind. Incoming governor Josiah Martin had to clean up the mess.

Closer to home, the residents around Snow Camp were no doubt devastated. Homes, farms, mills and livestock were pillaged by Tryon's forces. Many Quakers and Separate Baptists, having already been attacked by Regulators who disagreed with their pacifist stances, left for South Carolina or Georgia. The community divisions remained as the Revolutionary fires were stoked in the next few years.

What happened to Herman Husband? He fled north to Maryland, his birthplace, disguised as a minister. His wife, Amy, and children had already fled to Hagerstown in 1771, most likely around the time of the increasing tensions between the Regulators and Tryon's rising impatience with the Piedmont revolutionaries, in order to escape the vengeance of Tryon and the militia. Husband eventually moved to the Glades in Pennsylvania, where he cleared land and built a cabin. In 1772, he brought his family to their new home. It was there that Husband renewed his land ventures, and prosperity followed his hard work. Still, revolutionary ideas ran through his veins, and he joined a radical group in Pennsylvania. In 1778, he was elected to the Pennsylvania assembly. In 1794, he, along with other backcountry Pennsylvania farmers, became incensed over a new excise tax on whiskey, which was a major source of income for those in the western part of Pennsylvania. The farmers united, and their attacks, political and physical, were soon called the Whiskey Rebellion. Husband was captured along with several other men and twenty rebels. He died shortly after his release in 1795.

THE BACKGROUND OF THE WAR

The Revolutionary War in North Carolina began with the Battle of Moore's Creek in February 1776. (Some scholars call it the Lexington and Concord of the South.) Noted North Carolina historian William Powel points out that the battle prevented the British from occupying the southern colonies at the beginning of the war. Governor Josiah Martin was loyal to the British, and he devised a plan to invade North Carolina. The Crown approved, and plans were set to invade in February 1777. Martin thought the residents of North Carolina, such as the Highland Scots, were loyal to Britain. He had firm facts on which to base this conclusion. While North Carolinians protested unfair taxation, overall they still remained loyal to the King. But when the British developed plans to invade, this loyalty quickly dissolved. So Martin was wrong, and the Patriot Whig army defeated Martin's troops on February 27. The victory sent a new wave of enthusiasm throughout what would become a very divided colony for the duration of the war.

Once independence was declared, both in Philadelphia and North Carolina, those initially eager for war lost interest. In their eyes, independence had been attained. North Carolina troops were called out of the state to fight the British, and one of the battles was Valley Forge. From 1776 to 1778, North Carolina citizens were not involved in the war. But things were not as good for Georgia and South Carolina. Georgia fell in January 1779. South Carolina succumbed five months later. North Carolina was next in line.

Misled by the victories and Governor Martin's unflagging and naïve belief that the majority of North Carolinians were loyal to the Crown, Lord Charles Cornwallis set out to capture the Tarheel State in late 1780. After an embarrassing defeat at Kings Mountain in South Carolina, British troops fled to Winnsboro, South Carolina, to regroup. During this time George Washington sent former Quaker General Nathanael Greene to command the southern troops. Greene's strategy was brilliant: attack and then quickly pull back as if in retreat. It worked. After another embarrassing defeat at

Cowpens, South Carolina, Cornwallis, led more by arrogant pride than military sense, chased the enticing carrot of Greene's planned retreats into North Carolina.

Loyalists, people who supported the British during the war, were fairly abundant in the Piedmont, and this included the Snow Camp area and farther south. Cornwallis, still reeling from his embarrassing defeats in the western Carolinas, hoped to recruit Loyalists as militia. The locals knew the territory and could provide valuable information for Cornwallis and his senior officers. They served as guides and carried messages between the Loyalist ranks. They knew where provisions might be acquired, and most importantly, they knew where other sympathizers lived. Cornwallis made it to Hillsborough, where he planned to regroup and replenish his tired and demoralized army.

During this convalescence twelve miles north of Snow Camp, an embarrassing encounter between two groups of Tory soldiers was "fought," and it involved several Loyalists from Snow Camp. The history of this event is muddy, as accounts differ. Pyle's Massacre, also known as Pyle's Hacking Match and the Battle of Haw River, took place on either February 24 or 25, 1781. Quaker Dr. John Pyle, a former Regulator, was now a colonel in the Loyalist militia who lived near Lindley's Mill. He recruited between 300 and 400 Loyalists to join Cornwallis in Hillsborough. Leery of the local Whig Patriots who were nipping at Loyalists in the area, Pyle requested an escort for his troops for their march to Hillsborough. Colonel Banastre Tarleton led his British Legion unit of cavalry and foot soldiers to assist Pyle. Tarleton and his troops were feared because they killed their prisoners with swords. The gruesome deed had a name: "Tarleton's Quarter." His army included two cannons and 200 cavalry, as well as 250 soldiers. Undaunted, local Whigs pestered his troops as well.

Hearing of Tarleton's actions, General "Lighthorse" Henry Lee and his Whig force marched from Deep Creek to keep an eye on Tarleton. As fortune would have it, they met a man who gave them the locations of both Tarleton and Pyle. Lee, knowing that his Whig force's uniforms were nearly the duplicates of the Tories, convinced the locals that he was sent by Cornwallis to reinforce Tarleton's troops. Soon Lee's troops, swords raised high in the air, were riding alongside Pyle's soldiers, who thought they were reinforcements.

Here is where the story becomes cloudy. It is not clear who started the battle, but the swords the Whig troops carried were probably of lesser quality than military issue and so were not very sharp. The Tories, swords in sheaths, caught entirely off guard, were probably bludgeoned to death with the dull blades, thus the moniker "Pyle's Hacking Match." In the end, two hundred British lay dead.

As for Colonel Pyle, both he and his son, Captain John Pyle, were critically wounded. Legend has it that Colonel Pyle hid in a pond until it was safe to flee. Both survived and lived out their lives in Snow Camp.

Lord Cornwallis remained in the safe confines of a German settlement west of Haw River, slowly accumulating additional militia from the area. More skirmishes followed, including the Battle at Clapp's Mill on March 2, but he eventually caught up with Nathanael Greene's forces at Guilford Courthouse, which is in present-day Greensboro. General Greene's goal was not victory: he simply wanted to whittle down what was already a fatigued and disgruntled band led by Cornwallis. On March 15, 1781, the two sides engaged in battle. After two fierce charges, Cornwallis gained a Pyrrhic victory: Greene, as was his plan, retreated after a third and final charge to save his troops, but Cornwallis suffered many casualties, losing one-fourth of his army to death and injury. Cornwallis wisely realized he could not continue his trek to capture North Carolina, so he limped back to Wilmington. It was on this march that he paused in Snow Camp.

General Cornwallis in Snow Camp

One-third of Cornwallis's army was sick or injured. The rest were battle-worn and weary, and many trudged toward Snow Camp without shoes. Rest and food were needed. Cornwallis hoped that the neutral Quakers would take care of his army. Those who did not willingly do so were forced to provide their services.

News of his march preceded him. One account from a Dixon, Dickson or Dickerson family in the area (possibly Simon Dixon's family) illustrates how locals protected their property. One woman put her fine dishes and pewter in a wash pot, used grapevines to hold the handle and lowered it into a river to keep the Tories from finding it. She and her children hid in the woods for several days and lived off dried cornstalks. One person in the family was suspended from a tree limb or crossbar by his thumbs in hopes of torturing information from him.

Cornwallis's troops arrived in Snow Camp and settled around Simon Dixon's mill on March 22, 1781. Lord Cornwallis immediately commandeered Dixon's house, one of the nicest in the area, and ran off the family for the duration of his stay. The house of William Marshal, who sold farm goods to the Revolutionary army, was also confiscated. Simon Dixon was nowhere to be found, but his family took shelter in the mill. Anywhere from six to twelve soldiers who died in Snow Camp were buried in the Cane Creek Cemetery, and the wounded were placed in sling beds made by the locals. The beds, made of quilts or lengths of canvas, were hung from saplings or from horses. Anywhere from seven to one hundred "beeves" (as in "beefs," meaning cows; the traditions vary in number) were slaughtered along with 250 sheep to feed the men. One can imagine the pain of the locals seeing their main sources of food, including veal, milk and butter, as well as leather and tallow, not to mention money from sales, lost to the hungry men. Benches from Cane Creek Meeting were hauled outside and used as butchering tables. Until the meetinghouse burned down in 1879, members sat on these benches that still had ax cuts and bloodstains on them.

One story recalls that a local disgruntled farmer came to the camp in search of his cow. He was informed that, if indeed it had been slaughtered, he could get the hide. After he fired off a tirade against the soldiers, he was quickly removed from the camp. He did locate the cowhide but at a price: he was robbed of his new boots.

What is not clear is how much the locals provided in both the care and feeding demanded of them by Cornwallis. Was anything offered in genuine compassion? Warned in advance of Cornwallis's approach, Simon Dixon (or his sons; again the traditions vary), a supporter of the Regulators, disabled his mill and fled to Hawfields during the occupation. Dixon had once distributed fliers published by the Regulators and was afraid of repercussions. But others in the area were apparent Loyalists (or opportunists) who offered supplies to the hungry and semi-clothed troops. Eli Branson, John Pyle, Jonathon Lindley and James Allen turned in tickets to the British government to recoup their contributions after Cornwallis's departure. This was standard policy for Loyalists whose food and animals were taken by the army. Non-Loyalists received no compensation for their losses.

Two traditions linger from Cornwallis's brief stay in Snow Camp. First, General Cornwallis sat in an armchair by the fire for hours in the Dixon house, and this chair is now in the collection of the Greensboro History Museum. Second, according to an eyewitness known only as Mr. Pike, the British army brought two cannons, captured from Nathanael Greene's army, into Snow Camp. But, the story goes, the army did not leave with them. According to legend, they are believed to have been buried, possibly in the millpond. To this day, locals still wonder if the two cannons remain hidden beneath over two centuries of silt. Were they stolen? A more probable solution to the tale is that, tired of the heavy cannons impeding the march to Wilmington, Cornwallis had his men bury them to prevent local Patriots from finding them.

On March 24, Cornwallis and his men left Snow Camp to continue their journey to Wilmington. Left behind were devastation and memories. No doubt, stores of wheat were taken from the local residents. It is quite probable that commanders of lesser rank stayed in other homes while foot soldiers slept in the elements. Horses had to be fed, and this required hay. One permanent reminder of their stay is a rock wall constructed between Dixon's Mill and Cane Creek Meeting. A cannonball was found in the wall by locals in 1920. Grave robbers found several musket balls in the Cane Creek Cemetery. And, according to one tradition, Cornwallis named the area Snow Camp, apparently in memory of the snow (that may or may not have been there) that kept the soldiers cold for those two days in late March 1781.

General Cornwallis sat in this chair. *Courtesy of Snow Camp Historical Society.*

After the troops left, Simon Dixon returned home. He died a few days later. Some say he contracted camp fever, a common malady that took many lives in war camps. Others believe that he was tortured by Cornwallis, but this would have been impossible since the army had left before Dixon's return. However, Tory sympathizers in the area could have been responsible for his death.

The History of Snow Camp, North Carolina includes a song written by Simon Marshall Dixon, who was born in July 1813 and died in March 1881. The song was first published in the *Burlington Times News* on February 26, 1908, and then included in a manuscript entitled *Investigation of Local Resources for the Social Studies in Alamance County* in 1939. It is known as "Simon Dixon's Song" or "The Battle at Dixon's Mill Where Nary a Shot Was Fired." The lyrics are presented here in abbreviated form with some commentary. From these lyrics, we can see some of the culture of the time and the routines of encampment of an invading army.

> *It was March's twenty-second day*
> *That here the British army lay,*
> *Still covered with the bloody stains*
> *Greene gave them on old Guilford's plains.*
> [One of the main things that armies commandeer is horses]
> *Toward even'g, when the tails were done,*
> *A father thus addressed his son;*
> *"Go, thou, and with thy cousin John,*
> *Take all the horses to the lawn."*
>
> *A mile or two they took them forth,*
> *And loosing them had turned back north,*
> *Which was the way whence they had come*
> *And with the bridles started home.*
>
> *When presently there came in view,*
> *Three or four horsemen, dressed in blue,* [as to distinguish them from the British redcoats]
> *Who, when these boys they have espied,*
> *They called and said, "These bridles hide;* [bridles were a precious commodity then]

The redcoats are about your home,
And you they'll take your horses from."
Admonished thus they crossed a bog
And hid them [the bridles] *under an old log.*

[The sight of the redcoat army must have been overwhelming, as the next verses reveal]
Now soon they see from off a hill
What does their minds with wonder fill;
One seldom such a sight enjoys
As burst a sudden on these boys:

Long lines of redcoats streaming on, [actually many were in faded, dirty and bloody rags]
Their arms all glittering in the sun,
While o're their heads a warning high,
The British colors proudly fly…
[Accompanied by fife and drum as well as wagons and horsemen, three thousand soldiers course around the road bends]

…Prepare to camp upon the hill
That stretches northward from the mill.
Now as the host o're spreads the plain,
A band of men come down the lane—

Whose equipment caps and swords
Proclaim them all official lords.
Arrived at the mansion where they stop, [the Dixon house]
And nimbly from their horses hop…

The hill now groans beneath the tramp
Of thousands fixing up their camp;
They chose it for the fairest scene,
A promising wheat field clothed in green… [winter wheat is green before it ripens]

To ruin all they had desires,
So took the rails to make their fires,
And to build a spacious pen
That night to hold their cattle in—

Of which they took full many a score,
And slaughtered here but eighty-four.
As Cornwallis lay in the big stone house,
T'was here that good old Simon's spouse, [Elizabeth Allen Dixon]

After family went down the hill,
To take refuge in the fulling mill,
Thought to take solace of a smoke—
What woman wouldn't under such a stroke?

But disappointment was her lot,
She found her pipe she had forgot:
And though it was among the foes,
For to regain it up she goes;

And as she steps into the yard,
True at his post the watchful guard
Presents his bayonet, the triggers gripe [sic]*,*
Forbids her get even her old pipe.

She spoke: her words overheard,
Her lordship promptly interfered,
And grants her what she did invoke,
The privilege to take a smoke…

[It was not uncommon for women to smoke pipes in those days. After the soldiers stacked their guns, some went to the mill to grind wheat.]

…For the Miller when first their arrival was known
In stopping the mill let the lightering shaft down,
Which letting both stones entirely together,
Now the runner was held hard fast by the other…

[Despite the best efforts of the soldiers, after a half hour, they could not get the mill to work.]

…America's eagle flaps her wings at the story,
For Britain succumbed—the old mill got the glory:

They gave up the contest and proclaimed aloud,
They had not a miller among their whole crowd.

It may be said of the battle of Dixon's mill,
Their foes [sic] blood in rain English arms did spill,
They were forced to make more use of their legs
Than they did when they fought at the battle of the kegs [barrels of wheat].

Thus it could be said that one miller and a mill defeated Cornwallis's whole army in Snow Camp.

THE BATTLE OF LINDLEY'S MILL

When Cornwallis left Snow Camp in March, the area was still under attack. After General Nathanael Greene chased Cornwallis's troops to Fayetteville, the Revolutionary War in North Carolina was virtually over. All that was left were skirmishes between Loyalists and Patriots. In essence, it was a civil war between combatants who were once friends. Guerrilla tactics, hit-and-run attacks and harried skirmishes frightened the locals. As the confrontations continued, it looked as though the Tories were on the rise. Colonel David Fanning, a Tory, was enlisted to bring down the remaining Whigs and thus restore peace to Snow Camp. Fanning was a brilliant and daring military leader, and his reputation as a ruthless, vindictive warrior who took out his anger on soldiers and families alike struck fear into the Whigs. As news of his revenge passed from neighbor to neighbor, anxiety filled the homes. Pillage, murder and mayhem resulted as buildings were burned and women were ravished.

Receiving notice that the governor of North Carolina, Thomas Burke, was hiding in Hillsborough, what was then the temporary capital of the state, Fanning and two other leaders, Colonels Archibald McDougald and Hector McNeil, garnered their respective soldiers. Fanning led a force of local Tory militia and his own soldiers into Hillsborough after a long night's march. Sources disagree on the number of troops under his command, ranging from six hundred to just over one thousand. On September 12, the governor, a small retinue of advisors and approximately two hundred Whig soldiers were captured. The Loyalists, emboldened by whiskey, celebrated by looting and pillaging the village. It took some time to bring them to order—time that would prove costly to some of their buddies.

The next day, "the hardest-fought battle of the American Revolution in North Carolina" occurred in Snow Camp, as noted by Algie Newlin in *The Battle of Lindley's Mill*. Also called the Battle of Snow Camp, the Battle of Lindley's Mill was fought on September 13, 1781. The fight involved neighbors against neighbors, a scenario that played out again during the Civil War. North Carolina Tories, those loyal to the British, engaged the Whigs, those who fought for independence.

After the capture of Governor Burke, one Whig soldier escaped and ran west to Haw River to warn General John Butler, who commanded the Whig forces in Hawfields, that the notorious Fanning, hated and feared, was on his way. Butler quickly rallied his troops, probably numbering around three to four hundred, and prepared for battle. The goal: to stop Fanning's march south to Wilmington, where he would turn over his bounty to the British. The numbers favored the Loyalists, but the terrain and Butler's tactical planning favored the Whigs.

There were two routes—one that was circular and another that was more direct—that Fanning and his army could take from Hillsborough to Wilmington, and both converged at Lindley's Mill. Rather than attacking Fanning's forces as they forged the Haw River, Butler moved his troops to Lindley's Mill, where the terrain was more favorable to a surprise attack.

Fanning's troops settled on the east side of the Haw River on the night of September 12. At five o'clock in the morning, they commenced their march, leaving behind the potentially hostile Whig settlers. The fatigued army crossed the Haw River at Woody's Ford, the soldiers and prisoners wading across the shallow waters while the officers took the ferry. Most of the soldiers were local militia, so they wore civilian dress or hunting clothes. The six hundred or so Loyalist troops and the two hundred prisoners, watched closely by Captain John McLean and his small group of guards, followed a narrow path, making the line of people probably over one mile, with the captured Patriot soldiers bringing up the rear. Nearly all trudged on foot with the officers riding on horseback. Provisions were transported by wagons, and two cannons were also in tow.

They entered a predominately Quaker settlement that supported neither side. South of the Quaker enclave were increasing numbers of inhabitants who remained loyal to the British. If Fanning and his soldiers could make it through the Cane Creek area unscathed, they could seek safety in the friendly confines of the southern Piedmont. At ten o'clock on September 13, they arrived at the trap set by General John Butler and his Whig soldiers.

As the Tory soldiers walked along a hollow, the Whig troops, standing on the hill above, fired once the advanced guard passed by. The first volley killed many in the line, and Colonel McNeill, hit by several musket balls, ordered a retreat. This was immediately countermanded by Colonel McDougal. This order played into the hands of Butler's plan, which was to distract the front line and separate it from the rear guard, which was also under attack, so that the prisoners could be rescued from their guards. Both Colonels Fanning and McDougal were determined to keep the prisoners from the Whigs, even if it meant killing every one of them.

Fanning called for a retreat back to the prisoners, who were secured, possibly in Spring Friends Meeting House. The battle raged for four hours, and the Whigs most likely made strong advances. But the Whigs soon retreated, probably giving in to the threats that prisoners would be killed if the attack did not end.

Then the Tory army attacked the Whig soldiers from two fronts, hoping to split them up. The attack had the opposite effect as well: it left the Tory army divided. Given that one contingent of soldiers had to guard the prisoners, Fanning's army was now in three sections. This gave some advantage to the Whig soldiers.

There is no solid evidence regarding which side called off the battle and retreated. Nearby Stafford's Branch ran red with blood, according to rather romantic and glorified accounts. Colonel Fanning was seriously wounded, and it seems several local Loyalists provided medical attention and also a safe haven for Fanning. In the meantime, the Tory army rushed southward to Wilmington. Butler's troops followed in pursuit.

The dead and severely injured were left behind. Residents in the area, especially Quakers, immediately took the wounded under their care and also buried the dead. Depending on the size of the houses, families could care for one or several of the injured. Relatives assisted their families in the dressing of wounds and feeding these soldiers. A local Tory doctor, Dr. John Pyle, rushed to the scene to offer his expertise. He was later captured by Colonel William O'Neal and officially placed in charge of the injured. All totaled, the most dependable estimates are that 51 soldiers were killed and 150 seriously wounded. Over a span of maybe two days, the locals buried the deceased in graves surrounding the battlefield. Today, there are no markers indicating where they were buried. The wounded, despite their pain, were able to march with their armies.

One story from the Braxton family sheds some light on this incident and the plight of the locals during the war. Mary McPherson Braxton saw the Tory soldiers coming across a field. She rushed to turn out the horses to keep them from being confiscated. Then she scurried back to the house and gathered together valuables, such as money, important family and legal papers and silverware. She opened the trapdoor in front of the fireplace, placed the items in the potato cellar, reset the door and pulled a quilt over it. She then set the baby on the quilt. Meanwhile, Thomas Braxton rushed upstairs and hid between the chimney and the gable. The soldiers entered the house but had enough decorum to leave the baby alone. Finding nothing of any real value, they went to the springhouse, where they enjoyed the stored butter and fresh-baked bread and washed it down with milk. They then enquired where Dr. Pyle lived and went on their way.

From the Whig perspective, the battle was for naught. General Butler's objective of rescuing the prisoners failed. Stalled but not defeated, the Tory force resumed its march toward Wilmington and handed over its prisoners. In the larger scheme of the Revolutionary War in both North Carolina and the other colonies, the Battle of Lindley's Mill was insignificant. In essence, it served two purposes. First, the ego of the much-detested Colonel Fanning was satiated by the bold capture of Governor Burke. Second, it was a battle between local Whigs and Tories. A month later, General Cornwallis surrendered to General George Washington at Yorktown, Virginia. The American Revolutionary War was over. But the memories of the Battle of Snow Camp linger to this day.

After the war ended, the institutions that served to bring order and civil services in North Carolina fell apart. During the war, newspapers closed, schools shut down and churches discontinued services. After the war, conditions were no better. People were divided: Tories versus Whigs, Church of England Anglicans against other Protestants, neighbor against neighbor, gentlemen versus small farmers. The people of Snow Camp faced all of these adversities. Two institutions arose that changed these divisive issues: schools that would teach decorum and new churches that would preach morals.

CHURCHES IN SNOW CAMP

After the Revolution, the people of North Carolina were anything but religious. Itinerant preachers continuously bemoaned the spiritual emptiness and outright sinfulness of the Tarheel people. This was especially the case for citizens of the Piedmont. In the early 1800s, a wave of revivals swept through the area, including Snow Camp, and in the 1820s, many sinners and backsliders turned from their secular ways. Soon, new churches developed. Besides the Quakers, three other denominations were represented in the early years of Snow Camp: the Christian Church, Methodists and the Wesleyans.

Pleasant Hill Christian Church

According to church records and recollections, some of which vary, Reverend John Allen, a member of the Christian Church denomination, began preaching in the area of Snow Camp in 1783, and other ministers soon proclaimed the Gospel there as well. Many in the community were converted, and thus there arose the need for a meetinghouse. Soon afterward, Nicholas P. Barrons began preaching in the home of Martin Staley. Staley is a key figure in the initial life of Pleasant Hill Christian Church. He was a blacksmith, postmaster, millwright and wagon maker, and he owned much land. Martin and his wife, Eleanor Bennett, bore seven children: Haywood,

This picture of Pleasant Hill Christian Church is undated. *Courtesy of Lisa Cox.*

Mary, Elizabeth, Eliza, George Washington, James Madison and Sarah. By 1823, the church had organized with six charter members: Martin Staley; Shubal Evans, who lived with Staley and was learning the blacksmith trade; Susanna Tyson; Elizabeth Coble; Mary Murchison; and Celia Way. Meetings were held in a nearby schoolhouse, and in 1824, Martin Staley solicited subscriptions to build a church meetinghouse on his land. Some called it Ponds Meetinghouse because it was beside two ponds. The one-room frame building was completed in 1825, and either Reverend John Allen or Reverend Nicholas Barrons named it Pleasant Hill after the local school in the area. Reverend Louis Craven was the first consistently employed pastor. He served for a yearly salary of $9.80, considerably more than what other pastors made at that time.

In North Carolina and other parts of the Southeast, "camp meetings" were being held at this time. Shortly after the Pleasant Hill meetinghouse was built, a "tent meeting" was organized. The "tents" were simple cabins made of logs. Families came and stayed for days in their own "tent." Hiram

Vestal deeded land for a new "camp ground" near Pleasant Hill, and the old log tents were moved and a preaching stand was constructed. A brush arbor was also built around the stand to prevent sun glare. After a few years, the camp meetings, which lasted for days, ceased, but then protracted meetings were held for the duration of one day on the first Sunday in October.

In 1844, another camp meeting took place at Pleasant Hill on the Friday night before the third Sunday in August. Pleasant Hill member A.M. Way penned his memories of the camp meeting years ago, and Lisa Cox has collected them into the *Pleasant Hill Christian Church Notebook*. Way remembers:

> *A new brush arbor was built, new tents were built, my father's being in the northwest corner of the square. Oh, how anxious I was for the time to come when we would all move to the campground. As well as I remember the preachers were Joseph A. Murry, Alfred Apple, Lovick Lambert. The women used to shout very loudly at these meetings and sometimes men would shout. The 3:00 [p.m.] sermon on Sunday was the usual time for shouting to began [sic] and would last until meeting broke. My mother was a great shouter as so was my grandmother, and I cannot [condemn] it because I believe they were good women. These camp meetings were grand times for small boys for they had nothing to do but carry water and keep the hogs away. I don't believe I ever saw a happier time in my life.*

Because of a drought, there was no camp meeting held in 1845 in the Pleasant Hill area, but in 1846, the folks gathered once more in their tents and around the arbor stand. Way continues:

> *Every morning about sunrise Wm. Nelson would blow a small tin horn as a signal for the tenters to assemble at the arbor for prayer; a song would be sung, a prayer would follow and then they would go to the tent for breakfast. There would be four sermons during the day and night: at 9:00 a.m. a short sermon and a recess; then at 11:00 or 12:00 a big sermon by some noted preacher; dinner would follow the sermon; at 3:00 another sermon and then supper about sunset. At dark the arbor would be lit up with tallow candles for people did not use oil then. A man would be appointed to keep these candles snuffed. The exercise at night would often be kept up till the late hour. The order of exercises would usually be first a song by the congregation from the* Christian Companion, *a hymn book published by J.T. Lenay, then the preacher would read a hymn from this book, then*

he would read two lines and the congregation would sing them and so on till the hymn was ended, then a prayer would be offered up and the sermon would be next. An exhortation would almost always follow the sermon an alter [sic] call by some minister who would be called to follow.

If mourners came to the altar there would often be loud singing, shouting and clapping of hands that could be heard miles away; the saying, "as noisy as a camp meeting." The shouting would not always be confined to the arbor but would break out sometimes at tents or after the meeting would be over we would hear shouting in the neighborhood and we would take our song books out and sing for them…I once heard Alfred Isley…preach and could hear his words distinctly though I was at home setting by a window upstairs over a mile away.

I never saw any preacher use notes at any of these camp meetings. They used no instruments while singing and everybody took part in the singing that wished to. Some minister usually led the singing and there was no giddy young people invited up to the front to do the singing. I memorized almost all of the songs and often a preacher would sing a new song and then nearly everybody would learn it.

Jesse K. Cole sang the "Old Ship of Zion," Alfred Isely sang "There's a Happy Land," Rev. Neuse sang "In the Sweet Fields of Eden[,]" Ashbel Nelson sang "There is a Glorious Fountain," Shubal G. Evans sang "Show, Pity, Lord, Oh, Lord, Forgive," and Martin Staley's favorite was "Attend Young Friends While I Relate the Danger You are In."

The camp meetings continued until the Civil War broke out in 1861.

In 1827, Reverend John Allen ordained Shubal Evans and Benjamin May as the church's first deacons. Preaching services were held sporadically until 1829, when Reverend Martin Staley suggested that regular services should be held the first Sunday of each month. In its early years, the membership was twenty, but after a revival in 1832, the rolls quickly swelled until they reached around three hundred. Interestingly, it was not until May 1861 that a communion service was held, led by Reverend E.W. Beale.

Sunday school officially commenced in 1871. In 1874, discussions began concerning a new building, but it was not until 1881 that the decision was finally made, thanks to the urging of then pastor Reverend John T. Hall. The project was placed in the capable hands of W.G. Murchison, A.H. Way and Christopher Teague. In 1883, the simple one-room frame house was finished. A bell was purchased from the Oakdale School by Dr. D.H. Albright for the church. With pastor J.W. Holt residing, W.G. Clements, a visiting minister, gave the dedication sermon in September of the same year. The old church building was sold for $16.50, probably to be torn down and put up elsewhere as a barn.

Troubles erupted in 1902 when a member was accused of lying. His membership was revoked, and this resulted in a mass exodus of members. These disaffected people began Pleasant Union Holiness Church. The troubles followed the new flock, however. Soon after the new congregation was formed, the church split again.

Other modifications to the recently built Pleasant Hill Christian Church building soon followed. In 1908, a new recessed pulpit was added, Sunday school rooms and a new entrance were built in 1913 and pulpit chairs were purchased in 1916. By May 1925, two new Sunday school rooms were in place, and larger windows had been installed. In September 1947, pastor M.A. Pollard and his wife moved into the new parsonage, which was just across the road from the sanctuary. The parsonage was dedicated in 1948. Reverend Pollard was the first full-time pastor of Pleasant Hill Christian Church.

The flock faithfully participated in and supported the Christian Church denomination, not just locally but also regionally. Representatives from the Western North Carolina Conference gathered there on November 16–18, 1915. And on April 2 and 3, 1927, Pleasant Hill hosted the Western North Carolina Conference Young People's Conference.

In 1954, a concrete-block building, affectionately named "the hut," was constructed, and the facility was named after Henry J. Overman, a church member who was instrumental in leading Boy Scout troops that met in the area. Overman was the son of Andrew and Virginia Overman, and he was a respected educator. He graduated from Wake Forest College in 1928, and he returned to his home to teach at Sylvan School, as well as at Staley, Saxapahaw and Eli Whitney Schools. He organized two troops of Boy Scouts, and none of his scouts left his troops. In 1939, the Cherokee council honored his work with the Silver Beaver Award.

Overman died unexpectedly in 1940 after a brief illness, and the community mourned the loss of this young, energetic and kind man. At the time of his death, Overman owned a British flag that was given to him by the King of England. The flag was to be used in a ceremony marking the deaths of British soldiers in the area at Cane Creek Friends Meeting. Overman had spearheaded efforts to erect a monument in honor of these fallen troops. In 1941, Troop 46 gathered on Easter Monday to finalize Overman's dream and dedicate this monument. The British flag was raised behind the monument in the ceremony. The scoutmaster's dream had been realized.

The plaque on this monument reads: "A Memorial to British Troops who died in the Old Meeting House during Cornwallis' encampment here on his retreat from Guilford Courthouse march [sic] 1781. Erected by Troop 46 B.S.A. Henry Overman, Leader, who died before completing it."

The second sanctuary burned on February 1, 1959. Services were held in the hut while Reverend Thomas Shreve immediately pushed the congregation to move forward and rebuild. Leaning on the wisdom of Finance Chairman Twiman Andrews, the Pleasant Hill faithful worshiped in their new $130,000 sanctuary on May 1, 1960.

Today, Pleasant Hill Christian Church continues its ministry. The 140 current members have supported their pastor, Reverend Howard Spray, who has led the congregation since 1987. On Sundays, the members attend Sunday school and then morning worship as well as evening services. On Wednesday nights, there are activities for the members, and Monday nights feature two Bible studies. Pleasant Hill Christian Church also supports missions, domestic and abroad. It participates in local parades and honors veterans, as well.

ROCK CREEK UNITED METHODIST CHURCH

First known as Rock Creek Methodist-Protestant Church, the congregation now called Rock Creek United Methodist Church was born sometime around 1836. Edmond Engold, Milton Coble, John McPherson and Balaam Hornady helped organize the church. Balaam owned an extensive amount of land, and he donated a parcel of it to the church, which completed its sanctuary in 1845. The original sanctuary still stands today.

From its inception to 1900, the early pastors included Reverends Alson Gray, John Martin, James Stockard, W.C. Kennett and C.F. Harris. In the twentieth century, the following pastors served the church: Reverends John Garrett, W.F. McDowell, W.F. Ashburn, D.A. Highfill, T.M. McCulluck, William Pike, J.T. Ledbetter, George Holmes, John Burgess, H.L. Isley and Dr. George Brown.

The United Methodists historically have had several different sub-groups. In America, the Methodist Episcopal Church was organized after the Revolutionary War by Francis Asbury, who single-handedly put together what is today called the Methodist Church. As the clergy and especially the bishops in the Methodist Episcopal Church gained more power, some within the denomination disagreed with the progression. More Wesleyan in doctrine and worship, the Methodist-Protestant Church was organized in 1830. In 1939, the Methodist-Protestants joined with the Methodist Episcopal Church (the original Methodist Church in America) and the Methodist Episcopal Church South (an originally proslavery sect of Methodism established in 1844) to form the United Methodist Church, and Rock Creek was part of this merger.

Reverend Henry Lewis led the congregation in its initial years as a member of the United Methodists. Those pastors who followed were Donald Johnson, Jerry Bryan, Don Lewis, P.F. Newton, Ervin Houser, Lloyd McClelland, Michael Deal, William Presnell, Delmer Chilton, Alvin Horne, Michael Sykes, Walter Graves, Donald Johnson, David McHale, Steven Taylor, Nancy Sturvidant, Lyle Miller, Donald Gum, Bill Wolf, Bill Jeffries, James Bryan and Carson O. Wiggins.

The growth and ministry of Rock Creek Church can be traced in the renovations, improvements and additions to the original structure. From 1940 to 1941, a new floor was built. In order to attend to the spiritual growth of its members, an educational wing, complete with basement and heating unit, was added to the back of the church sanctuary. New pews, bathrooms and water were also installed. In the 1950s, a front porch for the sanctuary was constructed, and the weekly worship was enlivened by a piano given by L.B. Robbins, an organ donated by Leroy Pickard and carpet. Mrs. Patton McPherson donated the land for the parsonage, which was completed in 1960. Other improvements were made through the following years thanks to a trust fund set up by G. Talmage Swing.

In 1980, the Annual Conference of the United Methodist Church presented an award to Rock Creek Church for having the oldest church building with continuous worship in the district.

PLEASANT UNION WESLEYAN CHURCH

As noted above, problems arose in Pleasant Hill Christian Church, which led to some members leaving the congregation. Members from the Wright, Teague, Allred and Johnson families formed a new church, Pleasant Union, on May 7, 1902. By that fall, a sanctuary had been built. Reverend J.W.

Parker, from the Apostolic Holiness Church in Greensboro, was the first pastor. He left in 1905. The small congregation was allied with the Pilgrim Holiness Church and was on one of its circuits that included Bethlehem (see below), Pleasant Grove and Staley Church.

The history of the church is scant, but records do reveal how moral discipline was handled by churches at that time. Church leaders closely watched over the flock, and anyone who wavered beyond the fold was called before the church. For example, in 1906, John Pike was accused of "handling tobacco." His name was later removed from the church roll. In 1910, David Teague was accused of being a busybody and stealing lumber. He paid a fine of four cents to the church, and the matter was resolved.

Membership declined in the 1930s and 1940s until only two members remained: Julius and Gertrude Wright. When Julius died in 1946, Gertrude moved her membership to Staley Church. From that point on, the church was closed.

Then a new pastor, Reverend P.G. Irwin, arrived, and by 1960, he had reorganized the church to join the Wesleyan Methodist Church and reopen its doors again. The church building was repaired, and a parsonage was built. Reverend Irwin died in 1965. After the Wesleyan Methodist and Pilgrim Holiness Churches merged in 1968, Pleasant Union changed its name to Pleasant Union Wesleyan Church.

Structural changes have been the main focus through the last decades. New stained-glass windows were added in the 1970s, and in the 1980s, a fellowship hall and new classrooms were built. In the 1990s, older classrooms were also renovated. The cemetery, which had been closed when the church closed, was reopened in 1995. The original 1902 sanctuary was replaced with a new brick structure in the late 1990s.

Bethlehem Wesleyan Church

One result of the late 1800s revival movement that swept the nation was the International Holiness Union and Prayer League organized in Cincinnati, Ohio, in 1897. The organization quickly developed into a church and changed its name to the International Apostolic Holiness Church. Soon, its fiery message reached the Piedmont of North Carolina.

In 1898, a revival led to the conversion of seventy-five local young people in Snow Camp, and soon they became "sanctified." Sanctification is a sort

Tent revival at Bethlehem Wesleyan Church. Date unknown. *Courtesy of Bethlehem Wesleyan Church.*

of "second blessing" or "second baptism" that manifests in an emotional, life-changing event. This style of Christianity was not accepted by many Protestants, so these new converts were not welcomed into the local churches. Understanding this problem, Jennie Cox, Will Allred and O.L. Ruth organized a tent meeting in 1905. It was held on the land of Monroe Roach. Bethlehem Church was born from this tent meeting.

The first board of advisory consisted of Henry C. Wrenn, Monroe E. Roach, J. Wesley Ruth, Thomas B. Terry and John Andrew. Monroe Roach donated two acres of land for the new congregation, and sometime later, he and his daughter and son-in-law, Mr. and Mrs. Joe Pike, donated an additional four acres.

Through the years, the name of the denomination has changed, becoming International Apostolic Holiness Church in 1913, International Holiness Church in 1919, Pilgrim Holiness Church in 1922 and the Wesleyan Church in 1966.

On Sunday, November 30, 1958, the original wood building burned to the ground. Only a few pews were saved. Tradition has it that Paul Thompson, inspired by the tragedy, began the Snow Camp Volunteer Fire Department soon afterward. The congregation, led by Reverend Don Richardson, met in Sylvan School until the new brick building was completed. The first service was held on the first Sunday in July 1959.

After the Fellowship Hall was built in 1979, the church held an annual auction and bake sale. Cletus Moon was the auctioneer.

Pat Morgan, a member since she was born in the 1950s, shared some memories of Bethlehem Wesleyan Church. Her uncle, Alex Workman, was removed from church membership for "not living right." One pianist, Ava Brookback, had a stroke, and she lost control of her left hand. But she continued playing with just her right hand, and nobody could tell the difference. Pat also recalls one time in the 1960s, during Vacation Bible School, when the local sheriff's deputies busted a liquor still near the church.

INDUSTRY

While many think of "industry" as factories, the term is much broader than that. It covers any type of work, from household businesses to major corporations. Snow Camp has been and still is home to many forms of industry.

Farming has been the cornerstone of Snow Camp from its beginnings. Early farmers sowed wheat, corn and oats. Hay was actually wild grass "sown by nature," as one account recalled. It grew in various meadows. Hogs ran free, and when farmers needed to round them up for slaughter or sale, they had to be lured back home, usually with corn. Hogs were important not only for their meat, fat and skin but also because they ate the slop produced by families. Cows provided beef and veal, butter, milk, tallow and leather.

Today, farming is still a major factor in the economy of Snow Camp, and there are still a few farms that have remained in the original families for generations. A drive around the area reveals different crops: wheat, corn, hay and soybeans are the major ones, but cotton fields are also on the rise. Farmers also raise cattle, chickens and goats. Years ago, Will Kimball used to raise mules, the offspring of a donkey and a horse. Around the 1940s, a pair of mules commonly sold for about $600. He recalls that the donkeys were shorter than the horses so it was often difficult to get them to mate. Sometimes the donkey was put on a platform so he could reach the horse.

Tree farms are also prevalent around Snow Camp. Lumber is a big business, and log trucks pass through Snow Camp on a regular basis. Will Kimball used to cut and sell lumber in the early 1900s. Marion Teague

The old Dixon Mill. *Courtesy of Snow Camp Historical Society.*

worked one end of a crosscut saw for him. They loaded the logs and slabs on a horse-drawn wagon and then took them south to Liberty, which had a bigger sawmill than the family mills in Snow Camp.

Some farms go all the way back to the beginnings of Snow Camp. The lands have been passed down through the generations, and names have sometimes changed because of marriages, but the tie to the land of the original family still remains strong. One of these farms is the Lindley Farm. Joe Bill Lindley and his wife, Jane, can trace their family all the way back to Thomas Lindley, one of the first settlers of Snow Camp. Thomas Lindley also started Lindley's Mill. Through the years, the farm has changed hands, but it has remained tied to the Lindley family. Way back when, it had a tannery, and various crops, such as cotton, wheat and corn, were raised.

It can be safely said that much of the industry of Snow Camp centered on the flowing waters of Cane Creek. The first mill built on Cane Creek was that of noted Quaker Simon Dixon, who hailed from Lancaster County, Pennsylvania. Like many families in search of new environs, he came to Snow Camp in the spring of 1749, built a cabin on Cane Creek and then returned home for his family. He came back for good in 1751. In 1753, he built a gristmill that operated until the 1940s. As noted previously, General Lord Cornwallis and his troops stayed there two nights during the Revolutionary War.

Simon Dixon also ran a "trucking" business. Settlers needed supplies that were not readily available in the area, so each spring and fall, Dixon took wagons to Philadelphia, loaded them with goods and brought them home.

The oldest running mill in Snow Camp is Lindley's Mill, about seven miles east of Snow Camp. Lindley's Mill was constructed by two of the first settlers in the area, Hugh Laughlin and Thomas Lindley. These men and their families came from Pennsylvania. Hugh and his wife were only recently married. The mill was built on Lindley's land, and the dam was constructed on Laughlin's land. After Mr. and Mrs. Laughlin died, Thomas Lindley, the grandson of the original owner Thomas Lindley, bought out the Laughlin interest in the mill. In 1844, the mill was sold to Paris Benlow, who then sold it to Joshua and John Dixon. A succession of other owners followed, but the Lindley family eventually purchased and refurbished the mill, and it has been grinding organic grains for the last thirty-five years. At this writing, the ninth generation of Lindleys own and operate the mill.

Today, it is a specialty mill serving bakers, restaurants, distributors and processors. It mills wheat, rye, spelt and corn. Muffins, pizzas, pretzels, breadings and other items are made from Lindley Mills products. Wheat is purchased from North Carolina, Virginia, Ohio, North and South Dakota, Michigan, Illinois, Texas, Kansas and Nebraska. The wheat is tested onsite before being selected and shipped to the mill. Then it is blended with other wheat to make the final product. Lindley Mills has an excellent reputation for a niche market.

Other mills ground the grains of Snow Camp farmers. Information is scarce, but a few details remain for some of them. Just over two miles south of Snow Camp stood the mill of Jones Cantor. The mill was bought and sold several times until it was finally purchased by Wesley Ruth. He repaired the mill and ran it until around 1930.

Just off what is today called Coble Mill Road was Little Ward Mill, constructed by Stephen Ward in 1820. He hired Benjamin Way and John Overman to oversee the milling. In 1843, the mill was sold to John Coble, whose son Stanly Coble then ran the mill. After a dam break in 1847, a new dam was built, and a sawmill and new corn mill were constructed.

Thompson Mill was built on land owned by E.M. Teague. It was owned and operated by William Thompson. Millers often ran several businesses, and Thompson had a wool-carding operation, corn mill and cotton gin. He was also a noted gunsmith, perhaps one of only two in the county at that time. He crafted chairs as well.

Some locals specialized in the specific tasks of clothing and textiles. In the early 1800s, the Braxton family, like people all throughout the county, hired out for many services. They paid to have their wool carded, spun and even dyed. Colors included blue, made of indigo; yellow, produced from birch leaves; and red, from madder, an herb. Eleanor Newlin Guthrie was hired out to make a coat for the Braxtons in 1843.

In 1835, Cane Creek became the home of Cane Creek Cotton Mill, later named Holman Mill. Jesse Workman built the dam that supported the mill in 1833. The building itself was three stories tall, and the mill initially employed twenty-five people. Nearly one thousand stockholders purchased shares in the company and built the dam on four acres of land purchased from Peter Stout. John Thompson most likely brought in the first load of brick, which was made several miles away on the land of Charlie Ward. Some families, like that of Margaret and Daniel Pickard, moved to Snow Camp in order to work at the mill. Some workers lived in millhouses built nearby. All could purchase or trade for items in the store that was also part of the complex. In the 1850s, fifty women were employed, and most of them probably were hired because of their experience with spinning and weaving at home.

In 1885, the mill was sold to a man who then willed it and another mill to his nephews, the Holmans. Parts from the Cane Creek Mill were used to repair another mill in Orange County. In 1893, Lewis Scotten reopened the mill, which manufactured shuttle blocks and then whetstones. Soon the factory returned to its original purpose: knitting. In 1912, the mill closed. Years later, the Holman brothers, Robert, Lewis and Sidney, inherited the mill. Robert began milling flour there in 1920. He also ran a general merchandise store and post office. When the mill closed in 1937, it was replaced with a cotton gin.

Except for a few mountain counties and Cumberland County, Alamance and Chatham Counties were the leading producers of wool in the Tarheel State in the 1800s. One contributor was the Snow Camp Woolen Mill. The mill, established in 1886 by Hugh and Thomas C. Dixon, had a dozen or so employees who toiled twelve hours a day earning one dollar a day, twice the salary that the Holt mills paid in nearby Burlington. Nearly all residents had connections to the mill in one way or another. Locals raised sheep and brought the wool to the mill. Others made lye soap, a key ingredient in the fulling process where the wool was washed, pounded or boiled in order to fatten the fibers and therefore smooth out the coarse texture. Pork fat was mixed with lye in the bottom of ash hoppers. While

Snow Camp Woolen Mill. *Courtesy of Alamance County Historical Museum.*

traditions suggest that all the lye soap in the community was brought to the factory every May 1, it is more likely that soap was brought to the mill throughout the year. Some no doubt bought the wool produced by the mill to make their own garments.

Snow Camp resident Sallie Stockard recalled her experiences with wool in the 1880s. Her task as a child was to shear the sheep, card the wool and then wash it. After the wool dried, she rolled it and then took some of the rolls to Dixon's Woolen Mill to be woven into cloth and blankets. Other women in the area also wove the wool into cloth in exchange for some of the wool that they would weave for themselves. One of these women was Sallie Roberson. She was known as a specialist: she would weave to order, and payment was wool. She was known for a fancy Balmoral fabric (used for underskirts)—black with colored stripes—that was quite stiff and so tight that wind could not pass through it.

The mill produced several items: jeans, flannel cloth, blankets, knitting yarn and rolls of yarn that were used for stockings. Initially, only one-yard-wide cloth was available for purchase, but some remember the day that a larger loom was installed. After that, seamless blankets could be made. The mill produced ten thousand yards of black-and-white striped cloth that was shipped to the state penitentiary and was then made into uniforms for the inmates.

Snow Camp Woolen Mill did not serve only the locals. Customers came from miles around, including Sutphin, Saxapahaw, Mebane, Shallow Ford, Sandy Grove, Pluck, Sanford, Jonesboro, Hawfields, Roscoe, Hillsboro, Belmont, Julian, Kimesville, Richmond, Pittsboro and other places. Jeans, rolls of cloth, flannel, yarn, blankets and "very burry wool" were purchased and taken home.

There was a bit of pride in the mill as well. One 1890 advertisement reflects either lingering North-South prejudices or a simple fact of manufacturing excellence: "Farmers and Wool Growers will find it to their advantage to have their own wool manufactured at home rather than buy cheap, shoddy goods from the North."

In 1899, the mill's president was Eula Louise Dixon, who was the second female student to graduate from North Carolina State College (now North Carolina State University). The tradition that she was an extension agent may have some merit given her alma mater. She also managed a local farm. There were several later owners—Joe Dixon; T.H. Hornaday; Thomas McVey, who was superintendent of the mill from 1893 until 1910; and Bill Fogleman—until the mill was destroyed by fire in 1912.

The Snow Camp Manufacturing Company, also called the Snow Camp Foundry and Machine Shops, was established in 1842. It sold products to mills, farmers and craftsmen both white and black. These products included improved circular saws, threshers, cotton gins, smutt machines, corn shellers, straw cutters, cane mills and saw- and gristmill irons. It made castings of items from one-half pound in weight to two tons. The foundry also sold millstones and bolting cloths. Just next door, the Dixons operated a small store. Lacking any railroad in Snow Camp, transportation of both goods and supplies was hindered. Because of this, the foundry closed in 1886.

Eula Dixon. *Courtesy of Cane Creek Friends Meeting Historical Room.*

A ledger from the Snow Camp Manufacturing Company is noted in Troxler and Vincent's *Shuttle and Plow*. The ledger lists twenty-two blacks who either worked for the foundry or were customers: Robert Allen, Jack Archey, Sim Bartin, James Bass, Joseph Black, John Boles, Mebane Burnett, John Chavis, Peter Chavis, William Croker, Diner (Dinah) Dixon, Allen Foust, Hinton Gowings, Ned Hathcock, Mary Husbands, Sam McPherson, Aaron Thompson, Gabe Thompson (master moulder), Hiram Tinnen, John Weaver, Wesley Weaver and Isah (Isaiah) White.

A note about stores near the foundry deserves mention. Mills generally operated at crossroads and thus were excellent sites for other businesses as well. After a customer received payment for grain, he could stop by the store next door for supplies and then carry them back home on the wagon. Or he could trade grain for products at the store. Blacksmith shops were conveniently located by these clusters of businesses since horses pulling wagons might need shoeing for the return trip. In Alamance County, some crossroads complexes even had a seamstress, tailor, wagon maker, coach maker, dentist and physician. Schools could also be found nearby.

What could be purchased from a store? The Clover Orchard Store on Cane Creek stocked the following in the 1850s: groceries, dry goods, shoes and boots, hats, medicines, tinware, hardware, crockery, confections,

Two men at the old Allen Store. Date unknown. *Courtesy of Snow Camp Historical Society.*

stationery and cutlery. Store owners usually made two trips a year to markets in places like Petersburg, Norfolk and Philadelphia. At the old Floyd Coble Store, the customer could buy gas and oil or order goods such as stoves and hardware (and pick up a few good jokes as well), and then Mr. Coble would go to Greensboro to pick them up. (One night, a man tried to rob his store, and Floyd ran out naked to catch the thief.)

Fairmount Foundry was founded by Temple Unthank around 1850. It ceased operating during the Civil War due to a lack of raw materials. After the war, D.H. Albright, W.J. Stockard, Nathan Stafford and William Henley became operating partners in the foundry. John Durham, a local mechanic and cabinetmaker, was also part owner. He was known as "Squire Durham," which made fun of his family's lineage going back to Durham, England. James Griffin was also a part owner. His job titles included farmer, mechanic and machinist. While many locals worked for the company, a few employees from outside Snow Camp boarded in two small cabins. The foundry produced turbine water wheels, horse-powers (a machine run by one or several horses connected to it that produces power for other machinery), feed cutters, plows, wagons, threshing machines, cider mills and other items. Pig iron and wrought iron were hauled in from nearby Graham. A blacksmith shop on the site also served the community. Business was great because the South had to rebuild after the Civil War, and the foundry manufactured many of the key items necessary for the reconstruction.

An ad in the September 8, 1887 *Chatham Record* newspaper provides the following information:

> *Stafford, Henley & Co., Holman's Mills P.O., Alamance Co., NC, Proprietors Fairmount Foundry, Manufacturing Turbine Water Wheels of special merit, built so as to be used in or out of water-house, as desired.*
> *Also Grist and Flouring Mill Machinery, Circular Saw Mills with simultaneous setting head-block, both simple and durable and quick to operate; Horse Powers, foot Mortising Machines, Cutting Machines, Corn Shellers, Cane Mills, Mill Screws and Castings of various kinds. Repairing attended to promptly. Correspondence solicited.*

William Henley was a unique man. He was a millwright and foundry man. He invented and patented the turbine water wheel. He also, along with Eugene Cole, who lived in Charlotte, received a patent for a cotton planter. Henley supervised the construction of new mills in the eastern part of the Tarheel State, especially on the Haw, Trent and Tar Rivers. The foundry closed in 1900.

After the Snow Camp Woolen Mill burned, a new mill was constructed beside the old dam. Called the Snow Camp Roller Mill or Snow Camp Milling Company, it was formed in 1924 by Harris McVey and Charlie Durham. It remained in operation until 1976. The mill produced cornmeal and flour and had a satellite store in Graham. Kyle Kimball recalls taking his corn and wheat after harvest to the mill and bringing back meal and flour to use for food. At the time the mill closed, it was only grinding livestock feed for local cattle farmers. In its early years, Charlie Durham drove his family in the mill truck to meetings at Cane Creek Friends Meeting and picked up children from around the community.

With the rise of industry in Snow Camp, a better road than the existing dirt road was needed to handle the shipping traffic. Several men formed a company and sold stock to raise funds to build a plank road from Snow Camp to Fayetteville. The new road meant faster transportation of heavy loads of pork, flour, tobacco, sugar, cloth and other items that flowed in and out of Snow Camp. Construction of the whole 129-mile road began in 1849 and it was completed in 1854. Hugh Dixon surveyed the route. After grading a dirt road, stringers were laid and then crosspieces of two-inch-thick planks were secured to them. Stringers and planks were milled locally. Mileposts were installed and toll stations built. The toll was generally two and one-half cents per mile. Gurney Dixon manned the Snow Camp tollhouse. When the Civil War came, the road fell into disrepair and was never improved.

Snow Camp was not just home to many mills; other industry offered employment as well. Some farmers ran side businesses, and one of these was pottery. There were at least two potters in Snow Camp: the Loy family and John Thomas Boggs. Boggs used local clay, and his products were sold regionally. His shop closed in 1919.

The more significant potter as far as innovation goes was Solomon Loy, who lived on what is now Old Dam Road. He is remembered as one of the most important potters in the state. Solomon was born in England in 1805, but he later moved to Snow Camp. His son John took over the operation, and John's sons, William and Albert, continued the family business. They fired up earthenware and stoneware until the 1950s.

Loy used what was known as a down-draft kiln, and he operated what may have been one of only two such kilns in the state, the other being in Salisbury. He also used cobalt to produce blue pottery, which was decorated with loops and lines.

Leather was needed for many uses, and there were a few tanners in Snow Camp. William Patterson Stout was one of them. His father-in-law built a tanyard and gave it to him when he wed Jennie Dixon in 1877. His business, which was near Sylvan School, produced leather for everything from shoes to harnesses and continued until his death in 1929. He received orders from the superintendent of the Christian Orphanage in Elon College (now the Town

Left: Bag from the Snow Camp Milling Company. *Courtesy of Cane Creek Friends Meeting Historical Room.*

Below: Horse and buggy. Rider and date unknown. *Courtesy of the Cane Creek Friends Meeting Historical Room.*

of Elon), Chris Johnston, the City Meat Market in Ramseur, veterinarian J.P. Spoon and various other folks. He also made shoestrings and whips from the hides, as well as livery items such as halters. Based on his correspondence in 1919, he was apparently considering switching from bark to chemicals to color his hides. In the mid-1920s, he was using Rosman Tanning Extract, made in Rosman, North Carolina. He also owned a store just above Bethel Methodist Church. Based on canceled checks from the mid-1920s, he sold through his store or else ordered from other businesses songbooks for various community folks, as well as goiter medicine and hardware.

When the new telephone technology was made available at the turn of the century, Snow Camp was quick to connect to the switchboard. Eula Louise Dixon provided the initiative that led to the first switchboard, which was built in 1910. It was owned by several folks and operated in Murphy Williams's house, until it burned in 1914. Then the Snow Camp Mutual Telephone Company was incorporated on March 3, 1914, by David Thompson, James Roach, Caleb McPherson, Claude Coble, H.J. Tiny and William P. Stout. The investing capital was $50,000, and people could purchase a share of stock for $20.

The switchboard was housed in a small, two-story, two-room house built by locals on land donated by Claude Coble. The night operator slept there; only emergency calls were handled at night.

Service was offered weekdays from 6:00 a.m. to 9:00 p.m. On Sundays, the switchboard was only open from 8:00 to 10:00 a.m. and 2:00 to 4:00 p.m. All calls were to be under five minutes, but no calls could be made during thunderstorms. Rings were based on a system of shorts and longs. The monthly bill was typically fifty cents, but it could vary depending on any damages to the lines that might have occurred due to weather or vandalism. The phone system was especially helpful during the 1919–20 flu epidemic.

Noted operators were Wilma Griffin, Swannie Teague, Myrtle Love Hackney, Ed Stuart and Callie Green Hanford. A rate increase in 1927 led to the end of the operation.

Today, locals go to the Snow Camp Raygo gas station to fill up their cars and trucks, get some groceries, find a tractor pin and get lottery tickets. Long before this, people frequented Floyd Coble's Store, run by Claude Coble and his wife, Bessie. At that time, it also included the post office. People at Cane Creek Meeting thought Bessie was sinning because she drank Pepsi-Colas. After the Cobles, the Allens then built a store there. Lorraine Griffin took over the store after the Allens died and then sold it to Burton McBane

Above: Telephone stock certificate. *Courtesy of Cane Creek Friends Meeting Historical Room.*

Below: People in Snow Camp were quick to invest in new businesses. Here is another example of the business stock available. *Courtesy of Cane Creek Friends Meeting Historical Room.*

for $1,000. The post office used to be in that store as well. This eventually became the Snow Camp Raygo.

The "hub" of Snow Camp in the mid-1900s was Thompson's Garage, built in 1931. Locals know well the silver Quonset building (think of the semicircular barracks on the *Gomer Pyle: USMC* TV show). Paul Thompson opened the garage, and his son Ray took it over. Cars, trucks and farm equipment were serviced there. Many recall standing beside the old woodstove. The standard joke was that the men were keeping the stove warm. Ray's "girlfriends" were the pinup calendar girls stuck to the walls around the garage.

Paul Thompson organized the fire department in 1959, and the first firetrucks were kept in his garage until a permanent structure was built. Some say the decision to build the fire department came about after Bethlehem Church burned down. Every evening, the firetrucks were parked in the garage and then removed the next morning.

Today, industry continues. Much like John Overman, who went door to door in Snow Camp to cobble shoes for folks around 1900, small businesses are everywhere. Heating and air, electrical, construction, computers, hauling, well-drilling, grading, financial advice, tax preparation, locksmith and tire repair are just a few of the businesses that call Snow Camp home.

EARLY EDUCATION

The North Carolina constitution crafted in 1776 recognized the importance of education for its citizens. The legislature required the state to at least partially fund schools. Before 1800, over forty academies were chartered, and they were exempt from taxes. The charters of many of these schools allowed children of poor families to be admitted free.

Education in the old days was much different than it is today. In a farm culture, life is based on the ebb and flow of planting, harvesting, butchering, repairs, spinning, weaving, food preparation and preserving. Fields are plowed, seeds are sown and the cycle ends when the harvest is complete, only to begin anew. Father, mother and children were all involved. Studies came during the "down" times of the agricultural cycle. There was no real school "year," so students were measured by their skills rather than by how many days, months or years they had attended. The result was sporadic attendance and inconsistent learning. Donnie Way recalled attending school only four months out of the year. Many schools were quite small. One example of this was the Hunting Branch School of Snow Camp, which began around 1870. Originally a one-room log structure, it was eventually rebuilt as a frame building. The doors were open only four months a year. Along with this, schools came and went like the seasons. Fogleman's School offered lessons from 1885 to 1895, when it closed, but it was replaced by West Point School, which also dissolved when Sylvan Academy was reestablished.

Schools were often formed by families or churches. The pastor or a family member who had some formal education taught, and students were taken in for a fee. When school was in session, the "scholars" boarded in the home where class was held or in a nearby house. A.M. Way recalled going to school in the 1850s at Pleasant Hill School and boarding in a nearby house built by Martin Staley for his son. In southern Alamance County, several small schools offered hope for many students in the ante- and post-bellum years. Cane Creek held school in its church until a separate building was constructed. Isham Cox established a one-room private school near his home in the early 1800s, and his daughters taught there. In the late 1800s, the county took over the school, and the name of his school was changed to Oak Springs. After this change, an increase in students led to the addition of an extra room. Ellen Pickett, Mary Cox, Rodema Hockett, Sylva Branson and Matt Coble, among others, taught at the school.

Judging from the following information, operating a school was seen as a moneymaking venture. Between 1820 and 1830, before Pleasant Hill School, there were several small schools in the area. Young scholars could attend Sandy Grove, a brick building where a Mr. Kernutt taught. Not far away, Jesse Hinshaw taught in a house with a dirt floor. Joseph Way also built a schoolhouse and employed Robert Burnsides as the teacher.

Other schools came and went as well, and their teachers included Tillman Barker, Franklin Pierce, Rencher F. Trogdon, George M. Albright and Miles Hobson. It was quite common for a young "scholar" to attend many different schools and have many teachers throughout his or her education.

One reminiscence from Able M. Way, writing under the pseudonym "Cornhill," published in a local paper and included in the *Pleasant Hill Church History Notebook*, provides an interesting picture of school life in the early to mid-1800s:

> I have read a letter from an old man 84 years old who describes the schoolhouse in which he went to school as being built with poles daubed with red clay, and dirt floor, a log cut out and greased paper for window lights. He says he not only went to school with home-made [sic] clothes and barefooted but to Sunday school also that way. He said he wore home-made [sic] clothes until he was grown and began to teach, but it was not the case with me. I wore tow britches and flax shirts till I was 10 or 11 yrs. old; then I began to wear store clothes for Sunday. This was when John Smith taught a singing school at Pleasant Hill.
>
> The writer whom I mention, speaks of going to Sunday School when a young boy, but there was no Sunday School near when I was small. It was in the early '50 [1850s] when Sunday School sprang up nearby. The first

one I attended was at the Pinefield schoolhouse near Rocky River Church, and it was about five miles off. The scholars came early and stayed till nearly night. They bought their spelling and reading books and some of the larger scholars bought their geographies. I was next at a Sunday School at Mt. Zion, in Alamance County not long afterward and those two were the only ones I was at before I reached my majority.

Cornhill's story also demonstrates that in the early times, Sunday school was actually school taught on Sundays. For many students, Sunday was the only day off from farm chores. Churches recognized that in order to develop model citizens, children should be not only religious but also educated. It was only later that the modern version of Sunday school as a religious enterprise developed. Of course, in those early days, the divisions between religious and secular education were not as wide as they are today.

Pleasant Hill School began sometime around 1840. Thomas Allred, Jesse Pugh, Reverend Enoch Crutchfield and Frank Stout were the first teachers, and Stout taught nearly one hundred children at the school. Some of the first teachers were Dr. Durant H. Albright, Reverend Samuel H. Way, Edmund Teague, Cate (Uliss) Hinshaw, Oliver Fogleman, Dr. Robert Glenn and Baisley Glenn. In the 1840s, Robert Burnside (remembered as a good teacher), George Daffron and Elizabeth Nelson taught for the school, as did Oliver Vestal, Lucinde Freeland (another good teacher from Orange County), Riley Way and Durant Albright.

Around 1860, Bethel School opened its doors to students. Eventually, the school was affiliated with Bethel United Methodist Church. The log building was replaced with a new schoolhouse, which was moved later, only to be destroyed by fire. Noted teachers included Inez Foust, Novella Stout, S.A. Sharpe, D.H. Isley, Lonnie Foust, Irma Holliday, Annie Lindley and Wilma Griffin. When the school district was divided between Sylvan School and Eli Whitney School in the 1930s, the school closed its doors, and the building was converted to a house.

Patterson School was replaced by Kimrey School in 1876. William Kimrey donated an acre of land, and people from the community gave materials and labor to build the new school. Once it was finished, H.C. Stout was the first teacher, and he renamed it Oak Dale High School. The school changed names again in 1879, and in 1880, Professor J.A.W. Thompson took over leadership of the school. Soon it was renamed Oak Dale Academy. By 1882, courses in penmanship and calisthenics were added, and because of demand, the academy building was enlarged and more teachers hired. The

Pleasant Hill School. *Courtesy of Lisa Cox.*

curriculum offered ancient classical languages (Greek and Latin), as well as music and military instruction. A recitation building was added in 1885, and then a normal school (a school to educate future schoolteachers) was begun. At its height, Oak Dale Academy offered several modern buildings with blackboards, wall maps, charts and a complete library. The academy was a leader in education, possibly the best in the state at that time, until it was destroyed by fire in 1895.

SYLVAN SCHOOL

The one educational institution that has endured the test of time in Snow Camp is Sylvan School.

After the Civil War, the Quakers throughout the North sought to rebuild the devastated South, and one of the foundations of this rebuilding was education. Cane Creek Friends Meeting already had a school that had served the community for two years, but the building was deemed too dark to provide a proper education. With help from the Baltimore Association; Joseph Moore, who came from Earlham College in Indiana and was superintendent of Friends Schools for several years before going back to Earlham; and Cane Creek Meeting, Sylvan of the Grove Academy was originally constructed in 1866 on the site of Cane Creek Meeting, and by December, it had eight students. A monument in the cemetery of Cane Creek Meeting marks the original site of Sylvan of the Grove Academy.

Quaker academies offered courses that would be associated with high schools today. Students met quarterly and boarded in nearby homes. According to the Sylvan School history *The Sylvanian*, Moore offered sage advice to his teachers: "Go to your work with a LOVE for it…Look to the temperature and ventilation of your school rooms…Avoid late hours and much visiting…Repeat and illustrate until your pupils have a clear understanding…seek for suitable opportunities to praise, encourage, and commend."

The story of one former student, Simon Stephens, is quite interesting. After marrying Martha Morris and having two children, Simon

The first Sylvan School building. *Courtesy of Cane Creek Friends Meeting Historical Room.*

experienced continuous harassment from a local man. One night, fearing for his life, Simon shot the man. Believing the man was dead, Simon fled to the west. He wrote home often but mailed his letters as he was leaving one town for the next, thus ensuring that no one could track him down. Unknown to him, the victim survived. Had Simon returned home, he only would have had to pay $3.00 for the incident—$1.50 for carrying a gun and $1.50 in court costs.

In 1866, the Sylvan Grade Report included the following curriculum: reading, writing, composition and rhetoric, history, English literature, spelling, English grammar, arithmetic, algebra, geometry, trigonometry, surveying, astronomy, natural philosophy, botany, zoology, physiology, geography, political economy, Latin and music.

Allen Thomlinson served as the first principal from 1866 to 1868. Early teachers were R.S. Andrews, Mary J. Cox, Sarah E. Wilson, D. Matt Thompson, Lizzie Rice, Clarkson Blair and Della Newlin.

Soon Sylvan became the largest—indeed, the only—rural school in the state. Its annual enrollment was between 175 and 200 pupils who came from all regions in the state. It had a reputation as a disciplined school, and this trait was instilled through an innovative curriculum that included floriculture,

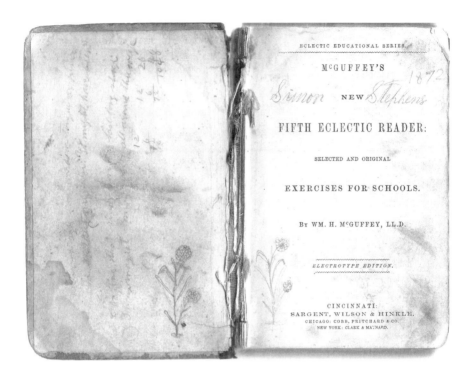

This *McGuffey's New Fifth Eclectic Reader* was published in 1857 and again in 1866. It belonged to Simon Stephens. Note the flower doodles. On pages 5–6, an 1837 fifty-cent piece was pressed into the page and then shaded in pencil on the next page to show the complete coin. A five-cent coin was likewise shaded on page 14. The *Reader* includes 201 stories and poems that contain valuable morals. These were taken from various sources, including the Bible. Each lesson included words to be memorized and spelled correctly, proper articulations, modulations and inflections of words and examples of improper pronunciations (to correct regional dialects that used terms such as "yit" for "yet"). *Courtesy of Sylvan Elementary School.*

debate classes, athletics, museum projects and trips into the nearby fields and woods. By 1903, it had outgrown its space near the Cane Creek Friends cemetery; a high school was added in 1908, and in 1910, it was moved to its present location on what was then called Flint Hill or Flint Ridge. Flint Hill was located on a road between Freedom's Hill Church and Pleasant Hill Christian Church that ran down by Dixon's Mill. Lucy Thompson, David Carter and Flora Stout were the first graduates in the class of 1910.

The "scholars" boarded in local homes or in the homes of friends. The homes belonged to the families of or were built by Moses Pike, Alfred Allen, Kate Shaw McBane, John Allen and Laticia Fogleman, Ralph Isely, Mahlon Dixon, Albert Foust, Floyd Allen, Thomas C. Dixon, Sam Tate and the Allens. Like students who go off to college today, many students only returned home on holidays or weekends. Students braved all kinds of weather when they walked or rode on horseback to school. A few had the luxury of arriving in a Model T Ford. Yet another innovative move from Snow Camp arose in either 1916 or 1917. A horse-drawn surrey driven by George Beale was introduced as the first school bus in the state.

Using money from a trust set up by Jane Allen Hammer (a graduate of Sylvan) and her husband, Isaac, land was purchased from Cicero Dixon, and a new building was constructed in 1912 out of bricks fired from clay mined from Finley Coble's land, which was adjacent to the school. The community lent its expertise, lumber, nails and muscle to construct the two-story structure that stood as a proud reminder of Snow Camp's care and concern for the educational well-being of students. Workers were paid from three to twelve cents per hour, and parents bought chairs for their children. For a brief period, the school was renamed Allen Hammer Memorial School. The name was not popular, so it was quickly changed back to Sylvan.

The new school consolidated many of the local schools. Students from Sylvan High School, Sylvan Graded School, Pleasant Hill, Oakdale, Center, Rock Creek, Flint Ridge, Gravel Hill Graded School and Lee Point all gathered under one roof for their studies. Other schools were added in 1930. A total of twenty schools were consolidated into Sylvan School. In 1960, high school students from Sylvan began attending Southern High School in yet another consolidation, and by 1974, all middle school–age children of Sylvan School were transferred to Southern Middle School. Today, Sylvan School only serves elementary students.

By 1927, the need for more space was evident, so an auditorium and five classrooms were added. A few years later in 1935 hot lunches were available for students. The price? Five cents.

The Sylvan Student Handbook for the school year 1950–51 contains pictures of the school and Principal A.M. Primm. A "Prayer for the Students" was included, along with a brief history of Sylvan School and the constitution of the student council. The grading system was covered (a D constituted failure), as was the curriculum for the full four years. Guidelines were listed for a pre-school clinic that was held each spring and administered by a doctor and county nurses. Rules for the cafeteria and the library were included. The school participated in the Red Cross, March of Dimes, Christmas Seals and Easter Seals fund drives. Other activities included the annual trip to Washington, D.C., clean-up day, Junior-Senior

Hammer School. *Courtesy of Cane Creek Friends Meeting Historical Room.*

Banquet, voice and piano lessons, glee club, May Day and the Four-H Club. In the case of fire, the students were instructed that "boys should be responsible for fire extinguishers."

Two tragedies are included in the history of Sylvan School. Many of Sylvan's teachers lived in the house known as the teacherage, which was next to the school. In December 1930, the teacherage burned. School superintendent C.V. Ferguson and his wife, along with eight other teachers, lost everything and had to be housed in local homes. The house was rebuilt, and today actors in the Snow Camp Outdoor Theatre summer productions room there.

In February 1974, the red brick Sylvan School burned to the ground. Eighth-grader Karen Thompson recalls looking out from her home and watching the building burn. But students were in school the very next day, thanks to the fast thinking and planning of school officials. Students were bussed to E.M. Holt School for several days until the gymnasium of Sylvan could be organized for classes.

Interestingly, as one looks at *The Sylvanian*, the history and picture book of Sylvan School, there are no black students in the pictures until after 1968, the year of the landmark case *Brown v. Board of Education*. This indicates that the school was segregated until after the end of segregation in the nation. Until then, African American students had to attend other schools, and this was often complicated. The first "colored" schoolroom in the area was built on land donated by Willie B. and Lola Hinshaw. The front wall was painted black and used as a chalkboard. It fell into disuse and was used as a barn until the building was donated to the Snow Camp Outdoor Theatre. There is another one at the intersection of Beale Road and Bass Mountain Road. George Walls recalls attending a local school before integration located on Road 49 south of Snow Camp toward Liberty. He also attended another mixed school in Randolph County for a while before returning to his first school. But eventually, black children all over Alamance County were bussed to Graham where they attended Central School, which had grades one though twelve.

Former teacher Bobbie Teague recalls that in the first years of desegregation, just two families with maybe five children initially attended

One of several "colored" schools in the Snow Camp area. *Courtesy of Snow Camp Historical Society.*

This house used to be a school building for local African American boys and girls. Another school is at the intersection of Beale Road and Bass Mountain Road. Old "colored" schools were often converted into barns, sheds or houses after they were abandoned. *Courtesy of the author.*

Sylvan School. One father was very anxious about his children. The oldest boy was predictably unhappy until he made some new friends. There were few black teachers in the early days of desegregation. Interestingly, there was one black male teacher at Sylvan in either 1915 or 1916. He was invited to teach an elective vocational education class in basket making. Students had to learn how to make splits. The students recalled no prejudice, and they respected their teacher, Passmore Burnett.

One former student remembered the first year of integration and seeing signs in the area that said "Whites Only." There was one black student in the whole school that year, and they became great friends. But after graduation practice, when they wanted to go out to eat and celebrate, the student's father said no, saying, "The closest you can come to a black is to say hello." This sentiment was also found in older Sylvan students, who were not so welcoming.

The first black students to attend Sylvan School who can be positively identified from *The Sylvanian* were Phyllis Compton, William Coltrane,

Sandra Staley, Milton Coltrane, Sheila White, Kay Harvey, Floyd Shoffner, Mark Shoffner, Gary Easterling, Darold [Darryl?] Coltrane, Dennis Patterson, Patty Foust, Delacey Coltrane and Ernest Shoffner.

Today, Sylvan School continues its legacy of being a leader in education as it quietly serves the children of Snow Camp. Funds from the Hammer Trust provide school items that range from physical support to school supplies to teacher assistants, which other schools in the county often have to do without. Using funds from a grant, Sylvan School recently opened a health center on its campus that serves both students and residents of Snow Camp.

THE PLEASANT HILL
TEMPERANCE SOCIETY

Riding the wave of the Second Great Awakening in the early part of the nineteenth century, several voluntary societies emerged throughout the young nation. They focused on the distribution of Bibles and tracts, a role for Sunday school and education and humanitarian causes, such as temperance. The basis for these societies was to provide grass-roots empowerment to change the ills of society and, indeed, remake society into the once-Puritan ideal that the nation was founded on. Snow Camp was no stranger to this movement, and the Pleasant Hill Temperance Society was the major voluntary association in the early years of Snow Camp life. The group served two purposes: first, as a social meeting that, second, centered around a specific cause. There were two other organizations in the Snow Camp area that fought against the misuse of liquor—Good Templars and the Sons of Temperance—but the Pleasant Hill Temperance Society was the most prominent.

It must be understood that alcohol was used for medicinal purposes by nearly all of society at that time, and drinking was also a cultural matter. For example, just a few miles to the west of Snow Camp, French, Scots, Irish and Germans settled and brought with them their propensity for drink. Soon, there were twenty distilleries and six stores that sold alcohol. Farmers also brewed their own concoctions for additional income. So when the Pleasant Hill Temperance Society was organized in 1833, its demand for total abstinence from alcohol was not popular.

Snow Camp was at the intersection of three counties in the early 1800s: Orange, Randolph and Guilford. The Pleasant Hill organization was born from the Hawfields Meeting House Temperance Society in Orange County. What brought about the new organization?

A large tannery in the area employed Stephen White, who, seeing his fellow workers getting "lively" from the abundance of liquor in the area, sought to remedy the situation. Helped by the Honorable John Long, an initial temperance society meeting was held in September 1833 in Hawfields. Twenty people, male and female, attended. One of those present was the "stiller," William Albright, who was also the postmaster of the Sandy Grove district. Convinced of his evil ways, he closed his bar, converted it into a store and joined the society. He quickly took action, and in November 1833, Albright, along with Hiram Vestal, created the Pleasant Hill Temperance Society. Initially, the society met monthly in the homes of members but also in Mount Harmon, Mount Zion Church, Hickory Grove Church, Union Grove, Cane Creek Meeting, Mount Pleasant, Lancaster schoolhouse, Cane Creek Cotton Factory, Rock Creek, Rocky River, Bethel, McMaster's schoolhouse, Duncan's schoolhouse, Tabernacle, Richland, Center, Masonic Hall and Moon's Chapel. Unfortunately, it is not clear if these were places or specific buildings. For example: Rocky River is a location that has a Rocky River Baptist Church and a Rocky River Quaker Meeting. "Bethel" could be the school or the church. This meeting schedule continued until after the Civil War, when membership dwindled and meetings were held twice a year, on or around the Fourth of July at Pleasant Hill Christian Church and then on Christmas Day at Cane Creek Meeting.

According to the early minutes of the Pleasant Hill Temperance Society, its goal was to "discountenance by precept and example the use of ardent spirit." Anyone above the age of fourteen could be a member. Those members who were caught using "ardent spirits" would be approached and given a chance for "satisfaction." If the accused did not confess, then he or she was "disowned" from the society. The use of "satisfaction" and "disowned" suggest a strong Quaker influence in the organization.

What were the immediate effects in the community? In a list of 345 members of the society from 1833 to 1839, only 10 were listed as "disowned," and 8 were erased from the rolls. Just as the society's members kept watch over their fellow members, Cane Creek Meeting appointed a committee annually to survey its own membership concerning their alcohol consumption. In 1844, the meeting minutes show that, except for those who used alcohol for medicinal reasons, out of 125 members, only 10 consumed alcohol.

The society celebrated its centennial in 1933, and 310 new members were added that day. Songs were sung, and a sermon by Reverend A. Plyer preceded dinner on the grounds, which was followed with an address by Honorable J.J. Hayes, a federal court judge. After special music, Professor Z.H. Dixon gave a historical address. Those present were particularly concerned over the passing of the Eighteenth Amendment.

The Pleasant Hill Temperance Society met for 109 years and is thought to be the oldest continuing temperance society in the nation. Led by the enthusiasm of Eula Dixon, a monument in its honor was erected in what is now the Pleasant Hill Christian Church cemetery.

SLAVERY AND THE UNDERGROUND RAILROAD

Marjorie Teague tells a story of an elderly black woman arriving at the Teague farm long ago. She asked if she could go and look at the old slave quarters down the hill. Marjorie was confused: she had never heard of any slave quarters in the area. But she did not want to ask questions that might suggest the woman was wrong, so she said yes, and the woman, who clearly knew what she was looking for and where it would have been, ambled off. Eventually, she came back. Marjorie asked if she found what she was looking for, and the woman answered yes. The building that now served as a chicken coop on the Teague farm was once used for slave quarters, according to the woman. As it just so happened, Marjorie was taking a bus trip with some others the following week, and so was the elderly woman. Marjorie went over and struck up a conversation with her. But, she noticed, the woman would not talk about slavery or the building at all. Nobody in the community knew that it had once served as slave quarters.

In the Piedmont of North Carolina, slaves made up 20 to 60 percent of the population, depending on the location. Most slaves lived on small farms. In Orange County, the slave population hovered around 29 percent from 1830 to 1850, and in the lower part of the area, the slave population was 1,356 in 1850. There were a few slaves in Snow Camp. Slaves that were sold in Randolph County in 1820 brought different prices depending on build, age, gender and thus potential: a male who was thirty-five years old sold for $200 to $300, while a fifteen-year-old girl brought $400, as she could produce more slaves. Thomas Braxton and his wife owned one slave named

Anthony, who was purchased for £150 (which might translate to between $400–$600) in 1814. Some slaves were buried in unlabeled graves in the cemetery of Pleasant Hill Christian Church with only blank stones marking the plots.

In the 1850s, there was a significant rise of slaveholders in the Piedmont, most likely encouraged by the new railroads that ran through Company Shops (now Burlington), just north of Snow Camp. This led to increasing racist attitudes among whites. With the railroads came new businesses and increased wealth, and one way to show wealth was owning a slave. Along with this, families often hired out their slaves to other families, who increasingly turned to black labor for menial yet backbreaking work. Most important, there was a class feud based on growing mistrust between white non-slaveholding farmers and wealthier slaveholders. Soon social, political, religious and personal divisions filled the homes, stores, churches and gossip of Snow Camp.

Politics were increasingly uncivil. A vicious political exchange took place in early 1860 between the powerful slaveholding judge Thomas Ruffin and John Stafford, who owned a plank road and manufactured iron agricultural

Does this stone represent a slave burial or an unknown member of Pleasant Hill Christian Church? According to Lisa Cox, member and historian of the church, nobody knows for sure. *Courtesy of the author.*

implements in his Snow Camp factory. Ruffin accused Stafford of collusion with the confrontational abolitionist John Brown and of being part of the Underground Railroad that was associated with Freedom's Hill Wesleyan Church, also located in Snow Camp. Ruffin reprimanded Stafford, who lodged Elder Adam Crooks and his associate Jesse McBride while they preached at Freedom's Hill. This placed Freedom's Hill Church and its members in the hotbed of the proslavery/abolitionist debate.

The topic of the Underground Railroad is a contentious one among scholars because documentation is often scarce, and what is available is often suspicious. One of the main issues is that much of the evidence is based on oral traditions, which, while interesting from a folk history perspective, are not reliable enough for the rigors of academic historians. One story hails from the Snow Camp area. According to Sally Stockard, who was born in 1869, some of her free black neighbors had arrived there through the Underground Railroad. This is difficult to verify, especially as two of her neighbors actually had free ancestors from the eastern part of the state. So were her black neighbors descended from slaves or not?

In 1805, in Greensboro, North Carolina, a young Levi Coffin, who attended New Garden Friends Meeting, saw a line of shackled slaves go by and was so moved with indignation and compassion that he, with the help of older cousin Vestal Coffin and other local Quakers, eventually planned an escape route to the north and northwest. According to later recollections, the term "Underground Railroad" was used first by Vestal Coffin's son Addison Coffin in 1819.

There is more evidence available for northern stations in the Underground Railroad, but it is nearly impossible to provide solid facts for it in the slave South. This is understandable. Because of the dangers of aiding and abetting runaway slaves in the South, the details of the Underground Railroad were stored away in the minds of the conductors and the owners of safe houses and the hearts of sympathetic church members. When they died, so did the stories. Still, there are enough bits and pieces to stitch together a fascinating—if tenuous—history of the Underground Railroad in Snow Camp.

In the Piedmont area, Quakers were torn over the issue of slavery. Should they oppose it but passively, a typical Quaker response to troubling issues? Or should they attack it openly? Many Quakers, ashamed of and frustrated by slavery and slaveholders, left the Piedmont in a mass migration to the northwest. But by the early 1800s, enough North Carolina Quakers had formed what historian Fergus Bordewich, in his book *Bound for Canaan*, calls "the only sizeable abolitionist community below the border states." Long established in the Tarheel State, their connections to family and friends in the northern states, aided by the exodus of Quakers to northwestern states, permitted them to offer a route to freedom for many slaves in North Carolina. Such was most likely the case for William Chamness, a Quaker who was born in Randolph County in 1802. He moved to Indiana in 1823, where he became a conductor in the Underground Railroad. He hid slaves under quilts and hay bales on his wagon trips to Canada. One wonders if his contacts back in the Snow Camp area were part of his clandestine emancipations.

There was also what is sometimes called an "overground railroad." Many Quakers bought slaves, officially freed them and then sent them or took them north to freedom. While seemingly altruistic, the practice was not without its critics for two reasons. First, since Quakers were against ownership of slaves, many questioned whether their purchase of slaves was an honest reflection of their beliefs. Second, some of the new "owners" often used the slaves until proper plans, connections and money were raised to begin their new life of freedom. For some, the idea was that the slaves would earn the price of their freedom, in essence paying back their "masters" for the initial costs.

Some Quakers owned slaves. Spring Friends Meeting met on October 29, 1842, to discuss member Oliver Newlin concerning his ownership of slaves. Guilty of owning slaves and marriage outside the Quaker family, he was soon disowned.

Sometimes, however, the situation was more complicated. Two examples are illustrative, and both involve the Newlins from Snow Camp.

The story of John Newlin is as unique as it is confusing. In *The Newlin Family: Ancestors and Descendants of John and Mary Pyle Newlin*, Algie Newlin calls him "possibly the most influential North Carolina Newlin of his day." Indeed, Newlin Township was named after him, possibly because he was the wealthiest person in that vicinity. He operated a tanyard that was once owned by his grandfather, and he ran a store as well near Spring Friends Meeting. He is best known, however, for his cotton mill in Saxapahaw. He and two of his sons, James and Jonathan, formed the partnership of John Newlin and Sons to operate a textile mill. He was, for a time, a Quaker lobbyist in the North Carolina General Assembly. He fought for legislation to make the emancipation of slaves less cumbersome. His reputation as an abolitionist and antislavery sympathizer was well known. But there was controversy surrounding his relationship with slaves.

In 1850, Newlin emancipated forty-two slaves in Alamance County. The story has several versions, and legal complications add more confusion. A

Sarah Freeman loaned her slaves out to Newlin when he built either his mill or the mile-long millrace in Saxapahaw. The agreement made between the two was that Freeman willed her slaves to Newlin and that, after her death, Newlin would then take the slaves to freedom up north. Freeman died in 1839, and the ensuing litigation lasted until 1851. Freeman's family (from her first marriage as well as her second) naturally contested the will. After all, forty-two slaves is quite a bit of property. The problem was, who exactly owned the slaves? Was the intent of the will carried out? Accusations were tossed about, including that Newlin sold his slaves in Fayetteville, hired them out or even let them live as if they were free when the law required that slaves live a slave life. Eventually, Newlin's actions were upheld as following the will of Sarah Freeman.

But was the move altruistic? There is no denial that Newlin used the slaves to construct his mill. Since it was often difficult to work out the logistics for freedom, sometimes these slaves were hired out (to pay for their upkeep) until they could be sent north. Thus, technically, some Quakers did indeed own slaves while standing for abolition. According to local accounts, it seems that the miserly John Newlin—his clothes were often worse than his employees', and he served poor food and paid low wages as well—went beyond this Quaker practice.

On the other hand, Nathaniel Newlin was an honest man, and a story of his purchase of the slave "Black Jim Guthrie" affirms this trait. Newlin bought Black Jim from Clabourn Guthrie, who was Nathaniel's brother-in-law, at an auction. Two of Nathaniel's nephews also owned slaves. When Nathaniel's brother Thomas returned home from Indiana to visit relatives, Nathaniel deeded Black Jim to him. This prevented unscrupulous locals from capturing Black Jim and selling him back into slavery.

It is clear from oral traditions and physical evidence that Snow Camp was part of the Underground

JOHN NEWLIN.

John Newlin. *Courtesy of Alamance County Historical Museum.*

Railroad in the years of slavery leading up to the Civil War. Cane Creek Friends Meeting was instrumental in the Underground Railroad. In 1823, the members agreed to assist in helping slaves flee to Ohio, Indiana and Illinois. As time went by, the meeting also agreed to cover the cost of sending ex-slaves to Haiti as well. The Friends assisted in the birth of Freedom's Hill Wesleyan Church, which also stood firm against slavery. At least one safe house in Snow Camp can be positively identified: the Kirkman House.

Today, the location of the Kirkman House would be just a few hundred yards south of Sylvan School on Sylvan Road. The house, owned by William Kirkman, once stood on land now owned by the Finley Coble family. Local tradition notes that it was not occupied at the time the Cobles owned it. Today, only a large rock marks the place where the two-story log structure was built. On the second floor, a dining area and an extra room gave respite for weary runaways during the night. During the day, when danger lurked, the slaves would hide in a hollow log nearby. The Friends at Cane Creek assisted with provisions such as clothes and food for slaves. Other antislavery sympathizers in the area may have also contributed.

But slaves had to be careful. How did runaways know if the safe house was indeed safe? Quilts were often the sign. It is well known that the "log cabin" pattern of handmade quilts (made up of a square in the middle and then strips around it until the desired quilt size was reached) was used to signal whether the house was safe. If the center block was black and the quilt was hung out at a particular house, it was safe; if the block was red, then it was not safe to enter the house. It is not known if this process was used in Snow Camp. Also, if runaways were at a safe house during summertime, then they had to pick vegetables throughout the garden, not just from one vine. Slave hunters knew from experience that if only one vine was picked, then this was a sign that slaves had hurriedly grabbed what they could before retiring to the house.

Another house may have also been a safe house on the Underground Railroad. Thomas C. Dixon built his new house about 1843–46 across the road from the Cane Creek Quaker Meeting House. Behind the new residence, a separate kitchen was built. This was a common practice in those days because kitchens often caught on fire. At one end of the kitchen was an expansive hearth to accommodate large iron cooking vessels. When descendants renovated the kitchen, they lifted up a large rug in front of the hearth and discovered four thick, wide, loose floorboards with the Roman numerals I, II, III and IV on them. Underneath the boards, they found a hollowed-out place that was four feet by four feet and deep enough to hold one human. Or a lot of potatoes. Or both. And there the story gets confusing.

According to family stories, the kitchen was a safe place for a runaway slave in the Underground Railroad, and this hidden, hollowed-out section would seem to verify this tradition. But the family also acknowledges that the place could have been used to store potatoes. "Root" cellars were often used by families to hold and keep vegetables (recall the story about Mary McPherson Braxton hiding the family valuables during the Revolutionary days), and many were underneath the houses. Some were accessible only by outside entrances, and the Allen House has an external entrance. Having a potato cellar near the hearth would mean that potatoes would be cool since they were in the ground and also dry since they were near the hearth; thus, they would last throughout the winter. The floorboards could have been numbered to show in which order they were to be placed, and the rug covered up the loose boards and added an aesthetic touch to the large kitchen. However, why would one place a flammable rug just a few feet from the fireplace where errant sparks could ignite it? Along with this, the use of numbers on the floorboards could indicate the need for a quick replacement of boards should slave hunters arrive in the area.

So, potatoes or slaves?

In the story "Incidents in the Life of a Slave Girl," which is in Henry Louis Gates Jr.'s *The Classic Slave Narratives*, Harriet Jacobs, writing as Linda Brent, described her struggles for freedom. When she decided to leave her master, a certain Dr. Flint, she found refuge in a house where the mistress was a slave sympathizer. The house had a somewhat secret room upstairs, and this is where Harriet hid. However, when Dr. Flint unexpectedly came to the house, she was rushed to the separate kitchen by the house slave Betty. A plank in the floor was lifted up, and Harriet hid inside the small hole. The slave girl then put the plank back in place and covered it with a buffalo skin and some carpet. Betty walked over the skin and carpet back and forth to distract Dr. Flint while asking certain questions. The questions were intentionally chosen to reveal information important for Harriet's escape. This scenario occurred more than once.

While speculative, this bit of information from a documented slave narrative provides a parallel that can be played out in the Dixon kitchen. Was a runaway slave kept in the Quaker family house until bounty hunters approached and then hurriedly whisked away to the kitchen? Only the winds of history and a few bits of recollections will ever know for certain.

White folks also used the Underground Railroad. John Randolph, a Snow Camp store owner, refused to serve in the Confederate army. In order to avoid persecution, he took the Underground Railroad to Norfolk, Virginia, and from there caught a ship that was headed north. He eventually made it to Ohio, where he cared for wounded soldiers in a hospital. Similarly, Confederate conscripts came to the Snow Camp area and booked passage on the Railroad to freedom from service in the Confederate army. One elderly Snow Camp resident and a free black man hid Confederate deserters. Privates Mullen and Isaiah Oberman used trickery to find out where and how the two men hid deserters. The two soldiers eventually discovered the two deserters plus another unidentified man, and they were taken from Snow Camp and placed in the Salisbury Military Prison.

There is also an oral tradition that Freedom's Hill Wesleyan Church, just a few hundred yards south of the Kirkman House, was part of the Underground Railroad. According to Dr. Bob Black, professor of religion at Southern Wesleyan University, runaway slaves were hidden in a hollow log nearby. Perhaps this was the same log noted in the Kirkman House story. Dacie Moon, who lived beside the church building, told the author that the church used to hide slaves under the building.

FREEDOM'S HILL WESLEYAN CHURCH

The story of Freedom's Hill Wesleyan Methodist Church is an important part of the Wesleyan Church. But its history discloses many important bits of information about Snow Camp as well.

The church has had several names in the past, including Freedom's Hill, Freedom Hill and Free Nigger Hill. The church was conceived nearly two decades before the Civil War by local pacifists who were both ashamed of and in disagreement with the proslavery stance of the Methodist Episcopal Church. Tired of the reluctance of local Quakers to aggressively fight against slavery, several people planned a new church to tackle the issue of slavery head on.

In the September 1847 meeting of the Alleghany Conference in Ohio, a letter was read from a small group of people in the Piedmont of North Carolina who sought a minister sympathetic with the plight of slaves. After the letter was read and a request placed before the meeting for a minister who would accept the challenge, a young Adam Crooks accepted the call. On September 21, the conference ordained him an elder.

Crooks was often mistaken for a Quaker wherever he preached. His reputation as an antislavery preacher preceded him, and upon arriving in a community where he was to preach, he was often assailed with cries of "abolition," "nigger thief" and "amalgamation."

The emerging North Carolina Wesleyan Church began in the Rock Creek and Stinking Quarter Creek area just west of Snow Camp. The Friends at Cane Creek Meeting worked with local sympathizers to organize

This picture of Freedom's Hill Church was taken after it was renovated. *Courtesy of Myrtle Phillips.*

the new Wesleyan church. Adam Crooks guided the disgruntled members of the Methodist Episcopal Church in the Piedmont to break away from their proslavery denomination. Elder Crooks initially preached "mostly to slaveholders" in the area churches, and since Quakers were sympathetic to his cause and ministry, he probably preached in their places of worship.

On the third Saturday and Sunday of December 1847, the first quarterly meeting of the Wesleyan Methodists in the Piedmont was held, most likely in a Quaker meetinghouse. Crooks preached in the door of the building and gave thanks for three parcels of land made available for new churches by local folks, one of which was Freedom's Hill. The twenty-three members of the new Freedom's Hill Church constructed their log building just a few hundred yards south of the Kirkman Underground Railroad station. The first trustees were George Councilman, Micajah McPherson and Alfred Vestal. Hugh Dixon and Margaret Williams witnessed the first deed.

The architecture, both inside and out, is interesting. The twenty-seven- by thirty-six-foot log church was built on land donated by Simon Dixon, a miller and a descendant of one of the first settlers in Snow Camp. Hand-hewn logs were held in place with wooden pegs. Wide, inch-thick, rough boards made up the floor, and the building rested on a foundation of fieldstones. There were two batten entrance doors, one on the front facing west and one on the north side, with flat, hand–wrought iron strap hinges. Handmade nails secured the door to the braces, and wooden shutters covered the windows. Hand-hewn benches with no backrests stood on wooden legs. Originally, there was no heat source for the building.

The pulpit was a raised platform of rough boards with seats on both sides. In the middle of the platform, at the front, rose a solid mahogany pedestal topped with a carved, circular Bible stand. On both sides of the Bible pulpit were similar pedestals topped with circular tables for lamps. Just below the pulpit, at the front of the church, was a mourner's bench. The bench was very thick, heavy and supported on wooden pegs that were not equally spaced apart.

Crooks's success in the antislavery cause was rewarded with intense persecution. A rising tide of discontent among Methodists in Montgomery and Stanley Counties emerged. Threatening letters were received. His effigy was tarred and feathered. To make matters worse, in April 1849, Crooks was arrested.

The folks in Snow Camp were caught in the middle of a theological and political uprising. Neighbor was pitted against neighbor. Crooks was banned from speaking at many churches. Proslavery supporters in the community regularly came by during worship services and fired shots at the church building. Eleven bullet holes were discovered in the walls when the building was restored, and the original front door has several bullet holes to prove the veracity of the story.

All was not well in some parts of the circuit, and the life of Freedom's Hill was in jeopardy. Crooks's life was chronicled by his wife, Elizabeth Willits Crooks, in her work *The Life of Rev. A. Crooks, A.M.*, and she included one reminiscence when Crooks recalled, "Two joined the Church, whom may God bless. The house at this place was threatened but I guess it stands yet." The effects of the rising fears of proslavery persecutors from Chatham County and Randolph had stymied the growth of the new denomination, and the congregation at Freedom's Hill was in danger of closing down. Crooks sensed the impending demise of the church. His post clearly indicates the imminent and escalating danger of the situation.

Thousands from Chatham, Alamance, Randolph, Davidson, Forsyth, Rockingham and Guilford Counties were planning to arrest him or even kill him. On August 2, 1851, just four years after beginning his ministry in the Piedmont of North Carolina, Crooks fled the Tarheel State. But after the Civil War ended, the church was born again. The last Wesleyan services were held in Freedom's Hill Church around the early 1900s. Locals still recall revivals that packed the Freedom's Hill building after it was formally closed. It was said that you could hear the praying a half mile away. People of all religious affiliations in Snow Camp attended the revivals there. Even after the church was closed, a minister still met with people for prayer in the building.

While the church was neglected from that time until 1973, it was somewhat of a local spectacle. It was located adjacent to Dacie Moon's farm. Moon's grandchildren used to play "church" in the abandoned building. Kyle Kimball, who lived just down the road from the Moons, recalls chasing rabbits inside it. The rabbits wriggled themselves up through the decaying weatherboarding into the building itself. The neglected structure was often frequented by vandals and derelicts from the nearby Damascus Home, a rehabilitation place for recovering alcoholics. Once, after a drinking party went awry, a fire built in the church got out of control and burned a hole through the thick floorboards. Fortunately, Moon discovered the fire and distinguished it before it destroyed the historic structure.

The building was eventually restored and then moved to a church camp in Colfax, where it fell into disrepair again. It was then moved to its new home on the campus of Southern Wesleyan University, where it was fully restored.

MICAJAH MCPHERSON

One of the most famous characters of Snow Camp is Micajah McPherson. Indeed, his very name brings mystique because people spell it differently: Macajah, Micajah, Macajar. Just as his name varies, so do the stories about him.

The story of Micajah McPherson, a fierce antislavery advocate, is an important one in the history of slavery in Snow Camp. McPherson was born on December 17, 1817, in Chatham County and was a Wesleyan Methodist. He was married with one son and two daughters. After Reverend Edward Smith, president of the Alleghany Conference, published an antislavery tract entitled "Love Worketh No Ill Toward His Neighbor," some copies made their way to Methodists in the Piedmont area of North Carolina. At this time, the Methodist denomination supported the institution of slavery, as did other denominations, such as the Baptists. Influenced by Smith's antislavery message, a small group of Methodists in Snow Camp realized that slavery violated the teachings of the Bible. The Methodists who broke away from their parent denomination formed a new one: the Wesleyan Methodists. Closer to home, local Methodists refused to accept the teachings and theology of their proslavery pastor, and some, including Micajah and his family, organized to become the congregation of Freedom's Hill. The new church, its pastors, its members and even the building itself became the targets of local proslavery advocates. Despite the persecutions of Reverend Crooks, who escaped for the North in 1851, and Reverend Daniel Worth, who came to Freedom's Hill six years later, McPherson and a few persevering souls remained at Freedom's Hill after all the other area Wesleyan Methodists closed their church doors.

McPherson is a somewhat legendary figure in the local traditions of Snow Camp. He is best known for a failed lynching, but details are confusing since there are five published accounts of the story. The first is by historian Roy S. Nicholson in a self-published pamphlet. Here is his complete, if a bit romanticized, version:

> *One morning as McPherson was about his work near the barn, a number of men road [sic] up and surrounded him. His escape from them was impossible, so there was nothing to do but await developments. He was notified that he was to be hung, but that did not cause him to recant. He was rushed toward a wood across the creek, while his wife and grandson who were watching him as he was led to his doom were helpless; they were alone and without weapons of defense. The only resort they had was to speak to God in prayer. As his captors led him away, one of them, to intimidate the wife and small grandson, fired a rifle ball into the house near where they stood. This frightened them but did not touch them. As he was led into the wood his captors began to demonstrate the sincerity of their threats. A few rods from the road, near a small creek, stood a leaning dogwood tree, with a fork about seven or eight feet from the ground, and slightly above a large rock. The mobocrats lifted him to the top of this rock, observing that a "knotty dogwood tree is good enough to hang a Wesleyan on," fixed the noose which they had improvised from a bridle-rein and shoved McPherson's body off into space. He soon lost consciousness, remaining so some time. After a while he realized that he heard steps, and listened. Faintly he seemed to hear horses wading a creek, and some one rode up and cut him down, remarking that he did not believe "the old rascal" was quite dead, but that they needed the noose to hang another.*
>
> *McPherson dropped to the ground too near death to move or speak. For hours he lay there helpless. Just before nightfall he revived sufficiently to begin dragging himself toward home on his hands and knees.*

According to another story, McPherson was accosted by a mob sympathetic with the slave owners. While his wife and grandchild Monroe Roach watched in fear and shock, the men took him away to be hanged on a tree. In a last act of intimidation, one of the men shot the McPhersons' house as well. Then they improvised a noose from a bridle rein and hanged McPherson on a nearby dogwood tree next to a creek. Satisfied that he was dead, the men left the scene. Later, some other men riding through the nearby creek spotted Micajah and, needing a rein, cut him down and left him for dead. Somehow McPherson revived and was slowly brought back to health by his wife. Today, Cane Creek Meeting has a piece of the dogwood tree in its Historical Room.

A third version differs slightly from the above account. McPherson's wife and *son* Monroe Roach watched as his abductors placed the noose around his neck and pushed him off a rock. Believing he was dead, the villains cut him down and took the noose with them.

The second and third stories raise important questions: First, why would Micajah's son be named Monroe Roach? Next, even if Phoebe, Micajah's wife, did stay home, why didn't she later search for him in the hopes of finding his dead body and bringing it back home? Even if she located him, could Phoebe have cut him down from the tree? Maybe she was not strong enough to complete the task, but surely there were neighbors nearby who would have helped. Or were they too scared to join her in the search?

The fourth version adds more confusion: McPherson was hanged by Confederates while his wife watched from their front porch. After they left the scene, she rescued her husband, who was not seriously harmed.

The area around Snow Camp was heavily influenced by Quaker pacifism, so antiwar convictions were strong there. Therefore, many young men refused to serve in the war and were chased down by "hunters," men hired by the Civil War leaders in North Carolina to capture conscripts and deserters. Interestingly, sometimes one chose to be a hunter in order to opt out of battle. This might have been the case for Snow Camp resident William Elisha Braxton, known as Bill. According to one account, men from the McBane, Braxton, Harris, Zachary and Perry families were conscripts who had fled. According to the Braxton family correspondence, Uncle Bill Braxton became a hunter to avoid going to the war front. Quite possibly, Braxton was chasing his own nephews. The more notorious hunters in the area included Washington "Wash" Luterlow and Osage Luterlow, Baker Edwards and "Gillam" Carter, father of Ellen Luterlow. Alfred Guthrie and two others were captured and taken to Raleigh, but they escaped. Wesley Harris was captured and sent to war, where he was killed. James Zachary and his son Seymore, probably captured by hunters, were in the army together.

This information provides a clearer picture of what happened to Micajah McPherson. Proslavery proponents in the area may have alerted the Confederate hunters as to Micajah's whereabouts. The locals surely would have been privy to Micajah's daily farm and milling schedule and possibly may have located him on the very day of his lynching. His wife and grandson Monroe Roach watched in horror (if the son Thomas, the person the hunters were after, had been there, they would surely have arrested him and left Micajah alone), and afraid to resist or to run for help because of the intimidating gunshot at the house, they initially stayed at home. Meanwhile, the abductors carried out their deed. With McPherson seemingly dead, the killers left, but caught up in the euphoria of their success and emotions, they later realized they had left behind the rein, so they rode their horses back and retrieved it. Afterward, his wife and grandson, having found him some hours later, took him home.

Still, one more question remains: why such violence toward McPherson, especially since millers were generally exempt from conscription? There may be more to the story. There were significant political and sociological issues surrounding the war in the vicinity, and these provide some informative background to the McPherson legend.

When Southern secession was in the beginning stages, a large number of residents in the Piedmont of North Carolina were pro-Union. When the state of North Carolina held a referendum on secession in 1861, the population was nearly evenly split. But in Alamance County, 293 voters were for secession while 1,101 were against. In nearby Chatham County, it was 283 for and 1,795 against. Guilford County was 112 for and 2,771 against. Randolph County had the greatest disparity in the Piedmont: 45 for and 2,466 against. Much of this was due to the pacifist Quakers and Moravians in the area. Randolph County (Freedom's Hill was in northern Randolph County at this time) was a major anti-secession region and home to many deserters, who hid in the Uwharrie Mountains. Several stories from Snow Camp illustrate the social complexities of this time.

First, some left the area for good. Amos Stuart's family recalls in their *Stuart and Allen Families* history, "Being a staunch Union man he deemed it most wise to abandon the South at the beginning of the Civil War, though it cost him fully 90 per-cent of all his possessions." Stuart resettled in Indiana in 1861. Others, however, like William Penn Lamb of Randolph County, worked to save their property and stay out of the Confederate army.

Second, young men from Snow Camp seeking to avoid conscription into the Southern forces had three options: join the Quaker denomination, pay a conscription "tax" or leave their homes to join the Union army stationed in New Bern, North Carolina. Predictably, there was a rush of men who desired membership in local Quaker meetings. These "War Quakers" were scrutinized carefully. Spring Meeting only admitted eight men in a time when it needed new members. Pacifists who desired to avoid conscription could pay a $500 fee to hire a substitute. Some left the area altogether. James Gilliam, from northern Chatham County, stole a horse from noted secessionist Stanly Coble of Alamance County. Gilliam rode the horse to meet his friends in the area of Cane Creek. Unfortunately, the horse fell lame, so Gilliam found someone who would swap him another horse. After the war, Gilliam offered to give his horse to Coble and pay the difference for the stolen horse. Coble refused and then sued Gilliam's mother, Sophia, who had offered the labor of her sons to pay off the full value of the stolen horse.

A few families were torn in two by the war. William Johnson reprimanded his grandson John Williamson for joining the Confederate army. Grandfather instead wished he had joined the Union forces. James Newlin, son of the John Newlin mentioned above, was a Confederate, while his brother, depending on the source, was either a Unionist or Confederate. Interestingly, Newlin's mill in Saxapahaw produced cloth that was used to make Confederate uniforms. Young Quakers were sent to salt mines, not the battlefront, to serve their time.

Some families in Snow Camp have ancestors who were veterans of the Civil War, and some of those survived Robert E. Lee's disaster in Gettysburg. These are buried in the Pleasant Hill Christian Church Cemetery. A few Civil War soldiers are buried in the Cane Creek Cemetery. William Newlin, grandson of John Newlin, was killed in the famous Battle of Antietam.

The story of Jesse Buckner, a member of Spring Meeting, is interesting. Initially, he enlisted in the Confederate army, but when he became sympathetic to the Quaker cause, he was stripped of his rank of colonel. Going home one night, he paused at the Spring meetinghouse. After meditating on the matter, he decided to become a Quaker. Spring deliberated for months before admitting him. Buckner then paid his fine. But, despite his paid fine, he was "captured" again because of the desperate need for troops and sent to a Confederate prison, where he was tortured. He refused to give up his convictions. He was sent home when his health had deteriorated. When his neighbors saw that his health had improved, they ratted him out, and he was imprisoned once more. When the war ended, he became a leading member of Spring Friends Meeting.

The Braxton family history, *William Braxton, Planter and His Descendants,* contains some more insights into the war. John Braxton, who served in the Civil War, wrote home on January 23, 1864, to assure his parents that he was well, despite the dearth of rations. Each soldier received a fourth of a pound of pork or ham each day to sustain him in hard duty. Money was the main issue, and all Southerners were affected by the devaluation of the dollar. Slave owners were hiring out their slaves for wheat, not money. John noted sarcastically that his eleven dollars a month was not worth fifty cents. He then complained that it was because of the large plantation owners and their slaves that the war was being fought in the first place. He concluded, "I do not think such men deserve their independence at all." In another letter to brother Hiram, John begged his brother to find him a substitute, saying, "Get one a little under eighteen and get him to enlist." The substitute was not procured, and John was killed in the Battle of Spotsylvania in the spring of 1864.

Other Braxton correspondence gives some general pictures of wartime. One local soldier apparently got out of his enlistment by carding enough wool to bribe his way out of service. James Thomas, from Snow Camp, was imprisoned. Farmers who originally were exempt from the war were eventually being forced to enlist. They all reported to a camp in Raleigh.

Families have oral stories of their ancestors' involvement in the Civil War, but some families are reluctant to talk about the times. This is an indication of just how volatile the social and political dynamic was between neighbors. Still, one oral tradition reveals Union sympathizers living in Snow Camp. A sick "Yankee" soldier arrived on his horse in the area, and the family of Peter Faust took him in. They hid him in their house and provided medical care for him as well. But he was too ill for a cure, and he died. The family quietly buried him in their church's cemetery and kept his weapons.

Not all antislavery and antiwar opponents were peaceful: in 1861 and 1862, John Helton (Hilton) led peace rallies in the Piedmont, but he also threatened to lynch all who supported the Confederacy. William Owens was more open to guerrilla warfare tactics to get his antiwar message across. Contempt, anger and violence emerged between folks who used to be friendly neighbors. Mistrust was so bad that Confederate sympathizers kept up surveillance against their neighbors. Frustrated with their thwarted attempts to capture deserters, known as outliers, many of the hunters resorted to violence: farms were ransacked, livestock was stolen, women were raped and children were threatened. Most important for this story is that, as William Trotter notes in *Silk Flags and Cold Steel*, grandfathers were beaten and tortured in order to make them reveal where their family outliers were hiding, and this relates to the Micajah McPherson story. As revenge, Confederates were the victims of guerrilla attacks by the outliers.

Perhaps this is why some residents in Snow Camp began to rethink their support of the war. On August 22, 1863, a public meeting was held at Pleasant Hill Christian Church. This is understandable after the defeat at Gettysburg the previous month. There was a large turnout, and led by M. McPherson, Reverend E. Crutchfield, Reverend S. McPherson and S. Stuart, a resolution, a copy of which is in the Pleasant Hill Christian Church History Notebook, was assembled. It stated:

> *WHEREAS, The time has arrived, and we have come to the crisis when every lover of peace, freedom, and happiness should express his sentiments freely and fearlessly, with an eye single to the best means of bringing the war to a close, which is now desolating and destroying everything that is dear to us on earth; therefore,*
>
> *Resolved, That we are in favor of any and every means that can be employed to bring about an honorable peace between the parties engaged as speedily as possible, without the shedding of any more blood, even if we must concede a part of that which we claim as our rights.*
>
> *Resolved, That we are opposed to paying any man one-tenth of our products, for we will not have it to spare, and we are also opposed to the law.*
>
> *Resolved, That we are for peace, and to that end the President is hereby requested to suspend hostilities, and propose a convention of all the States to accomplish the same.*
>
> *Resolved, That we fully endorse the course of* [gubernatorial candidate] *W.W. Holden in defending the rights and liberties of the people.*
>
> *Resolved, That these proceedings be published in the* [newspaper] *N.C. Standard.*

There is more. In the gubernatorial election of 1864, peace candidate William Holden was defeated. The outlier bands and their supporters turned to violence in their protests against suspected voter fraud. State troops were put on the alert in Randolph, Moore, Montgomery and Chatham Counties, places that just a few years before were the scenes of violence against Adam Crooks and his friends. Families of deserters were brutally tortured, even to the extent that those in favor of punishing the outliers for their dereliction of duty were embarrassed and appalled by the atrocities committed by their own more vindictive comrades. As the Civil War dragged on, there was an internal civil war in the Piedmont of North Carolina, with the state-sanctioned home guards battling the secretive but all-too-real "Heroes of America," who were antiwar Unionists.

Several Confederate grave markers are in Pleasant Hill Christian Church Cemetery. *Courtesy of the author.*

Thus, in the story of Micajah McPherson, there was more at stake than just a lone attack against a grandfather. Neighbors were afraid of what was happening to their community, their state and even their nation. Pro- and anti-Union supporters filled the pews of churches that tended to side with one faction or the other. Violence was rampant. The civil carnage was so fierce that, in the debates of the 1864 governor's election between pro-peace candidate William Holden and pro-war proponent Zebulon Vance, the latter made the tiny village of Snow Camp one of his stops on his tour of larger cities that included Fayetteville, Asheboro, Greensboro and Charlotte.

Interestingly, twenty years later, McPherson spotted one of his would-be assassins during a revival service. While McPherson held no grudge against his attackers, the ashamed man hurried from the service. McPherson remained a loyal Wesleyan until his death in November 1896.

SPORTS

Beginning around 1900, two sports have dominated Snow Camp—basketball and baseball—and the tradition continues. For about eight months out of the year, either the Sylvan School gymnasium or the Sylvan baseball field is full of athletes.

Sports played a major role at Sylvan School. In 1914 and 1915, the boys' baseball team won the state championship. In the early days of Sylvan High School, basketball games were played outdoors in all kinds of weather on a clay court until a gymnasium was constructed. In the 1950s, basketball was all the rage and talk of Snow Camp. From 1952 to 1954, the girls' basketball team won the Alamance County championship for three years straight with no losses. The five-foot-eleven guard Katrine Frye was chosen All State Girls Basketball Team in 1949, '51 and '52. Five-foot-eight forward Anne Fox also received All State honors in 1956. In 1958, the Sylvan girls were Alamance champions, again winning twenty-six games in a row. Guard Janet Pike, standing five feet six inches, was selected All-State that year. In 1947 and 1948, the boys' basketball team won the Alamance County championship. Tommy Stout, a guard on the 1952 Sylvan basketball team, was named All County in 1952. In 1959, the boys' basketball team emerged as the county's best team again, with a 13–2 record. High school sports ended in 1960 when Sylvan graduated its last senior class.

One of the cheers performed at the games was included in the student handbook: "Gonna dribble down the middle/Gonna shoot 'em up the side/gonna beat that team/gonna tan their hides!"

Reunion of the Sylvan High School girls' basketball players. Date unknown. *Courtesy of Sylvan Elementary School.*

Baseball was a major sport in Snow Camp, as it was in Alamance County, in the early twentieth century. Many mills in the cities had semipro teams, and the competition and pride was fierce. Some millworkers were even "traded" to work at other mills, just so they could play on that mill's team. By the 1940s, semipro ball was at its peak in the county, leading to a professional team, the Bees.

Snow Camp was no stranger to baseball. While the North Carolina Yearly Meeting of the Quakers condemned baseball, it is interesting that some Quaker men played local ball. For example, Tom Zachary, Algie Newlin, Clay Perry, Joe Perry and George Zachary, all from Spring Friends Meeting, played on the Saxapahaw team around 1910. Other local players included Seaton Quakenbush, Jardie Johnson, Sherman Laton, Ed Gilliam, Leland Perry, Bill Lindley and Coy Durham.

Baseball was an important part of the Sylvan School education as well. As early as 1899, the school fielded a ball team spurred on by cheerleaders. But for two years in 1914–15, the school baseball team was the pride of Snow Camp. The story begins with the consolidation of the many schools in the area into Sylvan School. Excellent players from the smaller schools were then on the same team. In 1914, players included Grady Clark, Randolph Buckner, Lewis Fogleman, Harry Stout, French Duncan, Oliver Clark, Harry Johnson, Allen Graham and Algie Newlin. Earl Williams was the team's manager.

"Little wonder that in 1914 the Sylvan Baseball team clobbered every team, won the Western Championship and went on to take the North Carolina State Baseball Championship," *The Sylvanian* notes with pride. On April 16, the battle for the Western Division began at 10:30 a.m. Sylvan shut out Gastonia 7–0 and then played Rocky Mount in the afternoon for the state championship. The game was "nip and tuck" for several innings, and after a rally in the ninth inning, the Sylvan team, "exhibiting plenty of ginger," defeated Rocky Mount in the eleventh inning 9–7. Discipline was the reason for the wins, according to *The Sylvanian*. For example, after one championship (it is not clear which one), the team disembarked off the train in Liberty (nine miles south of Snow Camp) and jogged back to the school.

The baseball team rode to games over narrow dirt roads in a two-horse wagon that was big enough to carry all ten players and their coach. One time, they left early in the morning in order to arrive in time for the afternoon game against the Hawfields team (approximately eighteen miles northeast of Snow Camp). On the way, they stopped at a "country store owned and operated by two well respected black men," according to *The Sylvanian*. Those who had some money went inside to buy some refreshments. The "happy-go-lucky" Lewis Fogleman bought a dozen bananas for ten cents. The principal, Blake Isley, scolded Fogleman: "Why you half-baked idiot: don't you know that bananas are the worst thing an athlete could eat. You won't be worth a nickel in this ball game." After belting a home run and crossing home plate, Lewis chided his principal: "That's what my bananas did for me."

In 1915, the baseball team won its second championship, defeating Raleigh 7–6. The game was played at the University of North Carolina–Chapel Hill. *The Sylvanian* said, "Fully 30 men from this place [unknown] and the Snow Camp section drove over to see the Sylvan boys win." This team's members were Grady Clark, Randolph Buckner, Lewis Fogleman, Harry Stout, French Duncan, Oliver Clark, Harry Johnson, Allen Graham, Lawrence Lohr and a player whose last name was Martin.

Some ballplayers from Snow Camp made it to the big show. Edgar Braxton was one. Born in 1900, he played with the Boston Braves in 1921. He pitched for ten years for the New York Yankees, Chicago White Sox, Washington Senators and the Saint Louis Browns. While with the Senators, he won ten and lost nine games in 1927. In 1928, he won thirteen and lost ten. That year, he had an ERA of 2.51, leading the American League. In 1929, he had a twelve and ten year. It was his last good year in pro ball. Braxton died in 1966 in Norfolk, Virginia.

John Carrol "Cap" Clark was born in Snow Camp in 1906. He attended Elon College, where he was captain of the baseball team, thus earning the nickname "Cap." During the Great Depression years, he coached at Raeford High School, but he went to the spring training camps every year in hopes of making it to the show. He played for the Philadelphia Phillies in 1938 for one year as a catcher. He later owned a sporting goods store in Fayetteville, where he died in 1957.

Glenn Perry lived in Eli Whitney where, as noted above, he played local ball. Glen had a "career" as a minor leaguer. When he was twenty-seven years old, he played one year in the Major Leagues for the Detroit Tigers in 1941 as a shortstop and second baseman. While his batting average that year was minimal (.181), he was better known for his fielding abilities. His family recalls that he just could not hit the major-league fastball.

Still, Perry played in the late 1930s in the minor leagues. He enjoyed his time with the Texas team the Beaumont Shippers, and one year they took the pennant in the Dixie Series. They also paid well: he made around $1,700 a year. He also played for the Buffalo Bisons and then the Newark Bears.

After his career in baseball, Perry settled back down in Snow Camp, running his family's dairy farm. He died in 1990.

Floyd Euliss Wicker played ball for Sylvan School in the late 1950s in the positions of pitcher and infield. He was in the last graduating high class at Sylvan. Tim Murcheson, from Liberty and a former major-league player for the St. Louis Cardinals and the Cleveland Indians, scouted him during his high school days. Floyd wanted to turn pro right after high school, but his mother had different ideas. So Wicker went off to play ball for East Carolina University. The team won the NAIA championship in 1961. He was the only freshman on the team that year. Once again, he was heavily recruited. He signed with the Cardinals, turning down offers from the Phillies, Giants and Orioles. He played in the minor leagues until he was drafted into the army, where he played ball as well.

Out of the army in 1966, he went back to the minor leagues. In 1967, playing with the Triple-A team from Oklahoma, he won the minor league equivalent of the Golden Glove award. In 1968, Wicker was called up to play for the Cardinals, who won the World Series that year. He batted .500 but only hit in four games. The following year, he played for the Montreal team, where he again was noted for his fielding skills. In 1970, it was back to the minor leagues, but soon he was drafted by the Milwaukee Brewers. In 1971, he played for Montreal and then the San Francisco Giants.

 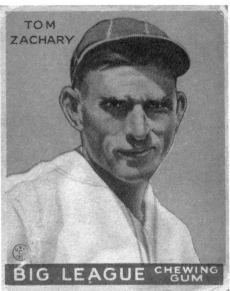

Left: Baseball card for Floyd Euliss Wicker. *Courtesy of Sylvan Elementary School.*

Right: Baseball card for Tom Zachary. *Courtesy of the author.*

Wicker usually pinch-hit in games. He spent most of his ten years in the minor leagues. But he played with some of the greatest ballplayers of all time: Stan Musial, Roger Maris, Willie Mays, Ken Henderson, Bobby Bonds, Willie McCovey, Tim McCarver, Orlando Cepada, Steve Carlton, Rusty Staub and Bob Gibson. He says Willie Mays was the best player he knew.

Wicker traveled all over the United States, Canada and even the Dominican Republic, where he played winter ball. After he retired, he raised chickens for a while and then delivered mail in Snow Camp for thirty-three years. Leaving the limelight for everyday life and work was difficult.

At this writing, he works part time at Sourwood Forest Golf Club. But he still gets mail from fans and autograph seekers. Some want biography information; others just want an autograph. Sometimes he receives large requests from dealers for autographed pictures, and he charges a fee for this.

Probably one of the most famous boys of summer of Snow Camp is Tom Zachary, who played major-league baseball in the 1920s and 1930s. Jonathan Thompson (Tom) Zachary was born in Graham in 1896. The son of Alfred L. and Ila Guthrie Zachary, he grew up a Quaker in Spring

Friends Meeting in Snow Camp. He attended Guilford College in nearby Greensboro, where he played football, basketball and baseball. He was a member of the Guilford College state championship baseball team in 1917.

In 1918, Tom Zachary, using the name Zach Walton, went to Philadelphia in the hopes of trying out for the Athletics. There are two different reasons he may have changed his name, and it is probable that both are true. First, the Quakers were against baseball (games were played on the Sabbath and thus a distraction from the holy day), and since his family were devout Quakers, he did not want them to know he was playing. (Though in his absence, how could they not know where he was?) Second, he was afraid of losing his eligibility to play college ball. The story goes that he stood at the fence watching the Athletics practice. He approached the coach and asked for a chance to try out for the team as a pitcher. When the coach asked how well he could throw the ball, Zachary replied, "Better than your pitchers can." He made the team, where he proved true to his word. He won two games and lost none in that season.

Toward the end of World War I, he had to enlist in the army. As a Quaker, he was a pacifist, but he served in France on the Quaker Red Cross unit until the war ended.

Standing six foot one and weighing 187 pounds, Zachary, who batted and pitched left-handed, resumed his baseball career in 1919 with the Washington Senators. In 1924, he helped the Senators win the pennant. He was traded to the St. Louis Browns in 1925, only to be traded back to the Senators in 1927. Zachary pitched against the legendary Babe Ruth in a game on September 30, 1927. Babe Ruth belted the lefty's curve ball for his sixtieth home run of the season, a record that was not broken until nearly seventy years later. Ironically, in the middle of the next season, Zachary was traded to the Yankees and roomed with Babe Ruth while on the road. He pitched two games in the World Series that year, leading the Yankees to the title of World Champions.

An interesting side note is that one family in Snow Camp has a baseball signed by the 1928 New York Yankees. Zachary's autograph is on the ball, along with a large signature by Babe Ruth.

Tom Zachary's major claim to fame, however, came in 1929. Zachary pitched twelve wins and no losses, a perfect season with an ERA of .248. No other major-league baseball pitcher has ever had a perfect season.

Zachary finished out his career with stints with the Boston Braves, Brooklyn Dodgers and the Philadelphia Phillies. All totaled, he pitched 3,126 innings over nineteen years and won 186 games while losing 191.

His career ERA was 4.93, and his batting average was .226. He pitched 3 games in two World Series and won all 3. When he retired, he moved back to Graham, where he lived a private life on his farm, tending to properties he had acquired over the years. He rarely referred to his baseball career but sometimes played in old-timer games.

Tom Zachary died on January 24, 1969. Today, a baseball park, Tom Zachary Field, honors him in Graham. It has hosted the American Legion Post 63 and Graham High School and Graham Middle School ball teams, as well as the Alamance Giants.

Baseball is not the only major sport in Snow Camp. Drive around, and you will see plenty of horses of all colors and breeds: quarter horses, paints, Appaloosas, bays, buckskins and roans. On the weekends, you may have to slow down and pass by riders on western saddles. But one of the best-kept secrets of Snow Camp is that two high-profile dressage horse riders and teachers reside in the area: Cindy and Eliza Sydnor. The mother-and-daughter team train and ride their horses at their five-hundred-acre ranch, Braeburn Farms, where the family also raises grass-fed beef cattle. Both have their own LLC companies. While many family members might not have a good relationship working together on a daily basis, the mother-daughter pair enjoy their time with the horses and each other. Each wants the other to succeed, and each understands her role in the business.

Cindy Sydnor wanted to work with horses all of her life and has studied, trained and competed in dressage since she was sixteen. Even though she has slowed down somewhat, she still competes, more to see how her horses are responding to their training than anything else. She mainly judges at many competitions throughout the nation (she holds the USEF "R" License), and she is a respected trainer who teaches at numerous weekend dressage events. She nearly made the Olympics in 1976, and she trained with the Olympic coach for several years afterward.

Cindy has lived in Europe and South America, where dressage is taught, and this led to her love for and training in dressage. While passionate for the sport and style, she is no snob, and this leads to a myth that needs to be dispelled: dressage is not an elitist sport. While every horse enthusiast will admit that owning a horse costs money, the glitz of the Olympics is misleading. Sure, top-level dressage competitors have to have money and even sponsors (it costs thousands to fly a horse overseas or across the country), but the average dressage participant might win enough money at an event to cover the gas for the ride home—or just a ribbon or horse blanket.

There is more to dressage than the fancy French name, which simply means "training," as in training the horse for whatever you need the horse to do. The style originated in Europe about five hundred years ago and is considered "classical" training. It started out in France, but Germany excels in the sport today, as do Russia, Denmark and the Netherlands.

Dressage takes a young horse between the ages of three and four and trains it according to its natural ways of movement, unlike other training, such as that of Tennessee Walkers, which is very unnatural for the horse. Dressage horses are gradually trained—initially about twenty minutes a day—and through the years, the horse is trained through four levels and then three more international levels. It takes a horse over nine years to reach this level of ability.

Cindy begins her training days early in the morning. One of her major approaches is to let the horses be horses. They are not cooped up in a barn; instead, they are allowed to range freely in the pasture. Working students keep up the barn, bring in the horses from the pasture, feed them a small amount of grain and hay and saddle up the horses, and then each horse is ridden. After the ride, the horses are allowed to cool down, and in summer, they are bathed, curried and then let back out to pasture. Training is six days a week, with one day off.

Eliza began riding around the age of four. She learned from her mother and has become a respected dressage rider and trainer in her own right. She has competed in local, state, regional and national events. One look at Eliza's website, and you see a talented and passionate horse-lover. Her resume of *major* accomplishments would fill a whole page. Here are just a few: participated in clinics with the gurus of the sport, such as Henk van Burgen, Scott Hassler, Jennifer Baumert, Gerhard Politz and others; won the Oldenburg Mare Performance Test to complement her other wins in this category, such as the U.S. Hanovarian Inspection; had several horses either win horse of the year or be selected to be featured in training events; worked with and trained with some of the best dressage teachers in the world; organized various groups such as the United States Dressage Federation "L" education program for judge training; earned instructor certifications, including the youngest person ever to be certified USDF fourth level; and the list goes on. She and her mom have been featured on DressageDaily. com, and she wrote an article for the online magazine as well.

The Sydnors hold several clinics on the farm each year, and they raise, board, stud and sell horses as well. If you stop by their farm off Bass Mountain Road (and you are welcome to at any time), you can watch and learn from some of the best dressage teachers in the nation.

WHAT TO DO IN SNOW CAMP

As we have seen, there is quite a bit of history in Snow Camp. But there are also quite a few things to do in the sleepy village of Snow Camp.

There are three restaurants in Snow Camp: Yesterday's Grill, Ye Olde Country Kitchen and George's Concession Stand.

Ye Olde Country Kitchen has been around since 1969, when James and Louise Wilson ran the restaurant. It was originally in the Snow Camp Raygo building next to the post office. The restaurant was moved to its present location when the Snow Camp Outdoor Drama, begun by Robert and Ruby Wilson, opened in 1974. The first year in its new location, it was known as Ye Olde Country Store. The building had nine additions before it burned in 1982. The restaurant was back in business the next year.

Bryan Wilson took over the Country Kitchen in 1987. He and his family now run the business, which has also expanded to Millstone Catering. The restaurant has been in the limelight. First, it has been featured on UNC Public TV as one of the best country restaurants in the state. *Our State* magazine picked the kitchen's fried chicken as the best in North Carolina. Food is not its only draw, however. One Hollywood movie was also filmed there.

Step inside for a taste of yesteryear. Coca-Cola antiques are everywhere, and John Deere toys are strewn about the place. Local wine and ciders are available as well as pies and breads. The Country Kitchen is best known for its buffet. The restaurant is open Thursday and Friday evenings and Saturday and Sunday for lunch and dinner.

Yesterday's Grill was opened in 1999 by Karen Thompson. She had experience in the fast-food industry, and she ran her own trucking company before taking a big gamble and opening her own restaurant. It was originally supposed to be a "party barn" with a pool table and drinks available. When Kyle Kimball asked if she was building a restaurant, she replied no but then thought that it was a great idea. Yesterday's Grill was born. Come by for breakfast, lunch and dinner, Monday through Friday.

For a unique eating experience, stop by George Walls's concession stand at the intersection of Coble Mill Road and Highway 49. It is just around the corner from Rock Creek AME Church. The fare is simple: burgers, hot dogs, chicken, fish, pork chop and bologna sandwiches and fries. Sodas are in cans or bottles. (In case you are wondering, he is a registered concessionaire, and his sanitation rating is excellent.) If George has a minute, you can ask him about the African American side of Snow Camp. But he is usually hopping from one end of the trailer to the other or taking orders on the phone. Place your order and then wait either in your car, under the trees or at the folding tables and chairs. As you wait, count the number of cars that drive by and beep their horns. Strike up a conversation with the others who are waiting for their food. You can find out a lot about Snow Camp over a burger and fries! Place your trash in the trashcan, and set your used cans on the ground beside it (somebody—nobody knows who—comes by and collects the cans).

George's stand is open Monday through Friday, 12:30 to 6:00, and Saturday from 11:00 to 5:00.

UNCLE ELI'S QUILTING PARTY

Every first Thursday in April, there is the Uncle Eli's Quilting Party in nearby Eli Whitney, just nine miles east of Snow Camp. The folks from Eli Whitney are quite quick to note that Eli Whitney is not in Snow Camp, so they claim the Quilting Party as their own. But the person responsible for Uncle Eli's Quilting Party was from Snow Camp, so the annual event can be included in the history of Snow Camp as well.

In 1921, noted local educator Ernest P. Dixon began a new high school in an abandoned cotton gin owned by Cal Thompson. The logical choice of a name for the school was Eli Whitney, after the inventor of the cotton engine (shortened to "gin"). In 1923, the school was moved to its present location in Eli Whitney. Dixon was a member of Spring Friends Meeting and lived from 1879 to 1953. He was known as a master teacher and the father of Eli Whitney School. The farmer and civic leader taught in the school system for thirty-two years, twenty-two of which were in Eli Whitney. A historical marker was erected in 1978 on the Spring Meeting lawn to commemorate Dixon's life.

In those days, quilters gathered to socialize as they crafted quilts. After a renovation to the school building, Dixon was looking for a unique way to get the public and the PTA more involved in the school. On the first Thursday in April 1931, he organized a quilting party that just happened to coincide with the PTA meeting. Quilters, parents, teachers and interested folks from around the area, including Snow Camp, came, and, except for one year, they have continued the tradition ever since.

In the early days, the quilters met for one big bee. A 1942 article in the farmers' magazine *The Progressive Farmer* provides a glimpse of the bee in its heyday. Seats were removed from the auditorium to allow room for the 75 to 100 quilters to set up their racks. Onlookers—as many as 1,000 to 1,500—watched as quilts were made. Needles were in full force as pieces,

Cleo Griffin at the Uncle Eli's Quilting Party. *Courtesy of Cane Creek Friends Meeting Historical Room.*

batting and thread were used to make a functional quilt that would one day probably become an heirloom. Lunch provided time for all to mingle, and some left in the afternoon to finish daily chores. All returned that evening for music, entertainment and to hear an invited speaker. Prizes were handed out for the winners of special categories of quilts. As the years progressed, the party became a place where local and regional quilters could come and display their craft or a quilt they had inherited or even bought. Today, the party even features other items. In 2013, one highlight was dainty embroidered handkerchiefs. In times past, hats and aprons were featured as well. The once community-wide event has now become more of a gathering of folks from everywhere who are quilters or those who are just curious about quilting.

Nannie McBane, a longtime quilter, has been attending since 1965 and is one of several local women who keep the tradition going. Local writer and historian Pat Bailey also spends a lot of time working behind the scenes to ensure the party continues. Quilts of all patterns and varieties can be viewed, as well as wall hangings and other types of stitch work. Some of the items are over one hundred years old, while others were crafted in the past year. Young and old alike share their creations. As expected, there are traditional patterns everywhere, but quilts featuring Native American designs, old T-shirts, feed and flour sacks and even old Crown Royal bags can be found. Visitors from Eli Whitney, as well as other parts of the world, have enjoyed the annual party.

There are no requirements or juries for the quilts and no rules for attendance. People bring their quilts and display them on racks in the old school gymnasium. Hundreds of folks attend each year. The event begins in the morning and ends with a picnic lunch at one o'clock in the afternoon. No tickets are sold, so just come on in. It is believed that this is the longest continuously running quilting event in the nation.

The Sword of Peace Outdoor Theatre

In 2013, the Snow Camp Outdoor Theatre celebrated its fortieth season. Who would have thought that there were enough resources and interest in the small community to create such a performance venue?

Sometime before 1973, Bobby Wilson was inspired by the stories of Snow Camp told to him by Ed and Lorraine Griffin. Soon after, he had

Entrance to the Sword of Peace Outdoor Theatre, also known as the Snow Camp Outdoor Theatre. *Courtesy of the author.*

an idea: why not build an outdoor theater and put together a drama about the Quaker resistance to the Revolutionary War? He presented his dream to Cane Creek Friends Meeting, and suddenly there was a groundswell of enthusiasm in the community. The Snow Camp Historical Drama Society was formed.

Bobby and his brother James Wilson were instrumental in the drama. The drama *The Sword of Peace*, written by the playwright William Hardy, premiered in 1973 on the outdoor stage. Two decades later, another play, Mark Sumner's drama *Pathway to Freedom*, portrayed the community's participation in the Underground Railroad. The music for the show was composed by Ann Hunt Smith. It is the only outdoor drama in the nation centered on African Americans and the Underground Railroad. The drama also offers a Broadway production and a children's play each season in the six-hundred-seat amphitheater.

The major actors and production crew come from all over the United States to participate in the shows. Local Snow Campians fill the minor roles. Over the years, many members of the Wilson family have been actors in the plays.

The grounds also features several historic buildings—a log house, Quaker meetinghouse, a "colored school," the old Snow Camp post office, a small general store and a small log meetinghouse—that provide an architectural panorama of local history. Visitors can also observe many antique farm implements.

Beginning in the 1980s and running for many years after, a Molasses Festival was held in either October or November at the Sword of Peace Outdoor Theatre. The festival drew as many as three thousand to five thousand people in its heyday.

There are some stories in Snow Camp that suggest Cane Creek was so named because of the sorghum cane that lined its banks. Molasses has been made in Snow Camp ever since its beginnings. The thick, brown liquid was used as a sweetener and in pies, shortbread and gingerbread. Donnie Way, who was an organist at Pleasant Hill Christian Church, recalls helping her family make cane syrup. Mollie the mule was used to turn the rollers that squeezed the sugar juice out of the cane stalks.

The festival itself was on a Sunday, but several days before, preparations were in full force. Cane was brought in, and York Teague's old press was put into use. The cane stalks were squeezed through two rollers, and the juice filled a small wooden bucket. The juice was then cooked for five hours to thicken it. Ten gallons of juice produced one gallon of molasses syrup. It was common to sell three hundred quarts of molasses at the festival.

Those who attended the festival were treated with music and could view the many antique farm implements at the theater. Apple butter was sold, basket makers displayed their crafts and period actors strolled the area.

The Bass Mountain Bluegrass Music Festival

Traditional music has been a part of Snow Camp for at least a century. String bands were popular in the Piedmont area. Many came from mill towns, while others consisted of families and/or friends. They played for picnics, school graduations, birthday parties and square dances, as well as other occasions. Just like other locations around the Piedmont, string band competitions were held at Sylvan School. Locals recall the Lattie (no one seems to agree on the spelling) Thompson family, whose six sons all played instruments—guitars, mandolin, banjo and fiddle—and performed for folks in the area early in the twentieth century. The band was very good and competed in competitions. They played at Sylvan School in competitions, as well as for entertainment, but no dancing was allowed in this Quaker enclave. One Snow Camp resident recalls that locals used to gather at Paul Thompson's garage for get-togethers and music.

Robert Eugene "Rob" Roberson recalled his teenage performing days in Snow Camp in the early twentieth century. His group played for house dances, and it was customary for a hat to be passed around to pay the musicians. The "pay" was minimal, but one time, the caller for the dance stole the money and was never seen again. Rob bought a banjo for five dollars and then went to a fiddling convention at Anderson High School. He won the banjo competition (because he was the only banjo player there!) and took away five dollars in prize money, enough to pay for his new instrument. In 1923, a large contingent of musicians from Snow Camp competed at the state convention in Raleigh. There were quite a few banjos and fiddles but possibly only one guitar in the group.

The guitarist might have been Donnie Way. Donnie played the organ for Pleasant Hill Christian Church. She was a self-taught musician, and one of her instruments was the guitar. In Donnie's early years, she noted that local students were hired by Dixon's gristmill to sew sacks out of cheesecloth for the grain. She recalls performing on the piano and guitar for the girls as they worked. She also played in a local band.

This musical tradition continues today with the Lil John's Mountain Music Festival. Each year around Memorial Day and Labor Day weekends, Snow Camp is host to several thousand bluegrass fans for three days who come to hear some of the top bluegrass acts of the past and present. In the fall of 1978, "Big" John Maness, along with his brother Pat (who was later tragically killed in an accident on the farm), held the first bluegrass festival. It has continued ever since and now is run by "Lil" John Maness II. Once known as the Bass Mountain Bluegrass Festival, the name changed to Lil John's Mountain Music festival in 2009.

John Sr., along with brothers Joel and Jeff and Mike Wilson, formed a band called the Bass Mountain Boys. Other players have performed with the band over the years. They played up and down the East Coast, as well as other parts of the nation. As Big John and the Bass Mountain Boys performed at other festivals, he brought back ideas for the Bass Mountain festival. Big John bought a farm in Snow Camp in 1976, and two years later,

Bluegrass legend Bill Monroe appeared at the Bass Mountain Festival in May 1983. *Courtesy of Natalie Maness and John Maness II.*

it was host to the first festival. Typical of the local propensity for industry, John worked several jobs in addition to farming.

Fans from every state in the nation, as well as across the Atlantic Ocean, have come to relax on the farm grounds and pick bluegrass. The brothers' mother, Linda, created the artwork for the festival. The park has had other events as well, such as tractor pulls and Halloween parties. Today, the farm is also Cane Creek Campground and RV Park.

When the festival began in the late 1970s, 200 to 300 people attended. Now the crowds range from 2,500 to 3,000. Performers such as Bill Monroe, Jimmy Martin, Marty Stuart, Alison Krauss, Ricky Skaggs, Rhonda Vincent, the duo Dailey and Vincent and others like Mountain Heart, as well as local bands, fill the venue. In addition to traditional bluegrass music, some more modern twists to bluegrass, such as pianos and electric basses, occasionally take the stage.

The grounds feature a main stage, with a side stage where bands sell their CDs. A mobile concession stand is brought in to serve large crowds. Folks camp in everything from primitive tents to popups to trailers to the large bus-like RVs. Most of those who attend are from fifty to seventy years of age, but the festival strives to bring in the next generation of bluegrass fans by offering workshops. During the day, people sit around and pick and grin in informal groups, share stories and trade guitar and banjo licks.

The campgrounds hosts visitors from everywhere. Salespeople, folks who are awaiting heart transplants at Duke Hospital or UNC Hospital, folks traveling through who need an overnight place to park and more traditional campers stay a day or more. But more than just camping takes place at the campgrounds. Horror scenes created by the Jones brothers of the Original Hollywood Horror Show (see below) have been filmed there.

The campground also has a bluegrass museum. The log building features old albums, playbills, pictures, rusted instrument relics and antiques that cover the walls. Some are for sale. Pictures of Big John playing the bass fiddle can be found. Old posters of past jams also decorate the walls. Every second Saturday, a bluegrass pickin' is held inside or outside the building. Campground staff grill up basic fare, and participants also bring dishes.

WOLFE WINES

If one digs around just a little, there is always a moonshine still in a family history or in the woods behind some old barn. That is the case with Snow Camp. Just a generation ago, there were at least three "hidden" within a mile of the author's house. Despite the best intentions of prohibitionists and temperance societies, it seems there will always be liquor of some variety or another. If for no other reasons, some need the spirits for "medicinal" purposes.

Today, the Piedmont of North Carolina is fast becoming wine country, and Snow Camp is no exception. Wolfe Wines, located on Snow Camp–Siler City Road, is the latest of many new wineries in the area. Floyd Wolfe runs a grading business, but he has also been making homemade wild blackberry wine for years. He shared it with friends, and the story goes that locals said it was better than other available products (such as moonshine). Charles Garner, a friend of the Wolfes, told Floyd to get off of his Caterpillar and open a winery. In 2008, Wolfe Winery was established.

The winery features wines made from local blackberries and various grapes. The list of wines includes: blackberry, raspberry, blueberry, cherry, apple, strawberry, kiwi, chardonnay, muscadine and merlot. Many of the bottles feature labels with drawings of local landmarks. On some weekends, you can catch live bluegrass music in back of the store. Come around Christmastime and try the cranberry wine.

THE ORIGINAL HOLLYWOOD HORROR SHOW

The Original Hollywood Horror Show is in Snow Camp. It is the only haunted house produced by true Hollywood filmmakers. The creation of brothers Dean and Starr Jones of Snow Camp, the show begins scaring folks from around the first of October through the first few days of November, depending on the calendar. It features the largest indoor horror facility in North Carolina and is one of the largest in the nation.

The Jones brothers are major figures in the Hollywood circuit. Their film credits number nearly two hundred features and even more television episodes. Some of the more famous include: *Star Trek*, *Pirates of the Caribbean*, *Day of the Dead*, *Night of the Living Dead 3D*, *Chain Letter* and *Train*.

Dean Jones is a writer, director and makeup artist who owns his own company, American Makeup and FX. He won two Emmys for his work on *Star Trek: Deep Space Nine*. He has worked on over seventy movies, including *Jarhead*, *Poseidon* and *The Santa Clause 3*, and over one hundred television shows in his career. He began his career experimenting with film and makeup while living in Snow Camp and received his BFA from UNC–Greensboro.

Starr Jones was inspired to become a makeup artist while attending the filming of a movie in the area directed by *American Bandstand* host Dick Clark. He received a book on makeup artistry one Christmas that sealed the deal. Like his brother, he began experimenting with makeup artistry for Halloween parties while living in Snow Camp. Starr was a Boy Scout and achieved the Eagle Award. Part of his scout work was making up wounds so that other scouts could learn about first aid. He also did makeup work for his high school plays. He went on to earn his BFA from UNC–Greensboro.

Starr's work has been seen in over eighty movies and over two hundred television shows. Some of his work includes *Day of the Dead*, *Toolbox Murders*, *Star Trek*, *The Abyss* and *Mortuary*. He also formed his own comedy troupe, the Kidneystone Kops. He has worked with famous actors, including James Earl Jones, Ellen Brysten, David Carridine, Lea Thompson and Ed Harris.

Many Snow Campians can be found in the cast and crew of the haunted house, which has over one hundred employees. People drive from as far as three hours away to experience the show. The brothers also film some segments of their Hollywood productions in the Snow Camp area, either at the Horror Show facilities, the Lil John's Mountain Music park or in other locales, such as nearby Graham. Be forewarned: the show is *very* scary!

SOURWOOD FOREST GOLF CLUB

Elmo Cobb loved to play golf, and so did his wife. So, he built a golf course, and that is how Sourwood Forest Golf Club began. Cobb began the project in 1989, and the course opened in 1990. The eighteen-hole, par seventy-two "country" golf course on Pleasant Hill Church Road draws duffers from all around, including Burlington, Liberty, Chapel Hill and Asheboro. Retirees frequent the course during the week. No pros have come from the Snow Camp links, but all who shoot for par at Sourwood know they are just a hole in one from the Masters.

Cobb originally did body shop work and then moved into landscaping, so he had a good idea of how to contour a piece of land. The workaholic has built three courses in the area: Southwick, Quaker Creek (he supervised the construction there) and Sourwood. For all three, he employed the same strategy. He bought the land, bulldozed and landscaped it, put in the first nine holes and opened the course up. Then he finished the last nine holes for the complete course.

Neil Matthews and Brad Fogleman operate the club today. The PGA course has a 73.4 rating with a 133 slope. It is open to the public and features various amenities, such as a pro shop, carts, putting greens and a driving range.

CONCLUSION

When looked at from a historical perspective, Snow Camp is a very big place. Much has occurred here over the centuries. Hearty pioneers left northern homes and staked out new lives in the pristine hills. Mills slowly ground grain, spun saws and ran machines. Huts and cabins were built. Religion thrived as folks attended meetings and went to church, built new buildings after fires or just to keep up with the times and brought revival to the backslidden and the faithful alike. Industrious entrepreneurs and creative, progressive thinkers were born in Snow Camp. Farmers still continue to weather the yearly storms and harvests. Movies are filmed, and music is played.

Stories are told of days long gone by. Armies and alliances and dissent and division among neighbors still linger in the minds of descendants. Tombstones and grave markers tell tales for those who pause long enough to listen. Genealogies provide links in chains that are many generations long. Memories of folks and events are shared with newcomers and family who return home to visit. Visions of what was rise up over what is becoming. Snow Camp has seen a lot of changes in its life. But the changes have not changed Snow Camp much, if at all.

Perhaps all should learn a lesson from the slow, bucolic life of Snow Camp. There is more to a book than its cover. When the life of Snow Camp is read, the past becomes alive once more.

BIBLIOGRAPHY

Allen, Beulah Oyama, comp. *Allen House and Some of Its Allens.* Nashville, TN: 1980.

Allen, John. Snow Camp Woolen Mill inventory from June 1894.

Bolden, Don. *Remembering Alamance County: Tales of Railroads, Textiles, and Baseball.* Charleston, SC: The History Press, 2006.

Boles, John B. *The Great Revival: Beginnings of the Bible Belt.* Lexington: University of Kentucky Press, 1972, 1996.

Bordewich, Fergus M. *Bound for Canaan: The Underground Railroad and the War for the Soul of America.* New York: HarperCollins, 2005.

Braxton, William L. *William Braxton, Planter and His Descendants.* Gwynedd, PA: Foulkeways, 1999.

Cane Creek Friends Meeting. *From Whence We Came: Cane Creek Friends Meeting.* Snow Camp, NC: self-published, 2001.

Carlin, Bob. *String Bands in the North Carolina Piedmont.* Jefferson, NC: McFarland & Company, Inc., Publishers, 2004.

BIBLIOGRAPHY

Celebrating Chamness Roots. Evansville, IN: M.T. Publishing, 2007.

Coble family records. Alamance County Historical Association, 1974.

Crooks, E.W. *The Life of Rev. A Crooks.* Syracuse, NY: Wesleyan Methodist Publishing House, 1875.

Euliss, Juanita Owens, Albert R. Shumate, et al. *History of Snow Camp, North Carolina.* Snow Camp, NC: Snow Camp Historical Society, 1971, 2005.

Gates, Henry Louis. "Incidents in the Life of a Slave Girl." In *The Classic Slave Narratives.* New York: Mentor, 1987.

Haines, Lee. "Micajah McPherson: A Laymen With Convictions." http://www.wesleyan.org/doc/assets/downloads/archives/down. php?dfile=Micajah McPherson.pd.

Hinshaw, Seth B. *The Carolina Quaker Experience: 1665–1985.* Greensboro: North Carolina Friends Historical Society, 1984.

Jeter, F.H. "Alamance Goes A'Quiltin.'" *The Progressive Farmer*, 1942.

"The John Allen House." Alamance Battleground State Historic Site.

Kars, Marjoleine. *Breaking Loose Together: The Regulator Rebellion in Pre-Revolutionary North Carolina.* Chapel Hill: University of North Carolina Press, 2002.

Lassiter, Mable. "Snow Camp Resident Recalls Early Days." *Mebane Enterprise*, February 25, 1971. Copy in the May Memorial Library, Burlington, NC.

Letters of Wilma Griffin. Cane Creek Friends Historical Room.

Mobley, Joe A., ed. *They Way We Lived in North Carolina.* Chapel Hill: University of North Carolina Press, 2003.

Moon, Milton. *Moon: A Colonial Quaker Family.* Cincinnati: John S. Swift, printer, 1996.

Newlin, Algie I. *The Battle of Lindley's Mill*. Alamance County, NC: Alamance Historical Association, 1975.

———. *Friends "at the Spring": A History of Spring Monthly Meeting*. Greensboro: North Carolina Friends Historical Society, 1984.

———. *The Newlin Family: Ancestors and Descendants of John and Mary Pyle Newlin*. Greensboro, NC: self-published, 1965.

Nicholson, Roy S. *Wesleyan Methodism in the South: Being the Story of Eighty-Six Years of Reform and Religious Activities in the South as Conducted by the American Wesleyans*. Syracuse, NY: Wesleyan Methodist Publishing House, 1993.

Pleasant Hill Christian Church History Notebook. Pleasant Hill Christian Church, Liberty, NC.

Powell, William S. *North Carolina Through Four Centuries*. Chapel Hill: University of North Carolina Press, 1989.

Smith, Laurie. "History of Pleasant Union Wesleyan Church." Unpublished paper.

Snow Camp Historical Drama Society. *The History of Snow Camp, North Carolina* (2006 ed.). Snow Camp Historical Drama Society, 2006.

Stuart, Elbridge Amos. *Stuart and Allied Families: A Genealogical Record*. New York: American Historical Company, Inc., 1938.

Sylvan School. *The Sylvanian: A History of Sylvan School*. Snow Camp, NC: self-published, 1980.

Teague, Bobbie T. *Cane Creek: Mother of Meetings*. Greensboro: North Carolina Yearly Meeting of Friends, 1995.

Trotter, William R. *Silk Flags and Cold Steel: The Civil War in North Carolina: The Piedmont*. Winston-Salem, NC: John F. Blair, 1988.

Troxler, Carole Watterson. *Farming Dissenters: The Regulator Movement in Piedmont North Carolina*. Raleigh: North Carolina Department of Cultural Resources, 2011.

Troxler, Carole Watterson, and William Murray Vincent. *Shuttle and Plow: A History of Alamance County*. N.p.: Alamance County Historical Association, Inc., 1999.

Various websites were also researched for this book.

INDEX

A

Abigail Pike historical marker 36
African Americans 79, 96, 97, 105,
    127
Alamance County 14, 15, 22, 31,
    40, 42, 79, 88, 89, 96, 106,
    118, 119, 125, 126
Albright, D.H. 81
Aldrage family 21
Aldridge, Buddy and Nancy 29
Allen, Alfred 93
Allen, Elizabeth 58
Allen family 23, 84
Allen, Floyd 93
Allen, James 54
Allen, John 15, 27, 36
Allen, John, II 25
Allen, John, III 25
Allen, Rachel 27
Allen, Reverend John 66
Allen, Robert 79
Allred family 69
Allred, Will 71

American Revolution 18, 32, 45
Andrew family 41
Andrew, John 71
Andrews, Twiman 68
Archey, Jack 79

B

Barrons, Nicholas P. 63
Bartin, Sim 79
baseball 18, 125, 126, 127, 131
basketball 18, 125
Bass, James 79
Bass Mountain 16, 18, 139
Bass Mountain Bluegrass Music
    Festival 138
Bass Mountain Boys 139
Beale, George 94
Bethel United Methodist Church 89
Bethlehem Wesleyan Church 70, 86
Black, Joseph 79
Boggs, John Thomas 82
Boles, John 79
Branson, Eli 54

Braxton, Edgar 127
Braxton family 37, 62, 76, 120
Braxton, Hiram 120
Braxton, John 119
Braxton, Mary McPherson 62
Braxton, Thomas 103
Braxton, William 19
Braxton, William Elisha (Bill) 117
British 31, 45, 51, 52, 53, 54, 56,
    57, 60, 67, 68
Brookback, Ava 72
Brown, Dr. George 68
Brown family 21
Brown, John 105
Brown v. Board of Education 96
Buckner, Jesse 119
Buckner, Randolph 126, 127
Burlington 15, 76, 104, 148
Burnett, Mebane 79
Burnett, Passmore 97

C

camp meetings 64
Cane Creek 15, 16, 21, 22, 23, 31,
    32, 34, 35, 37, 39, 50, 60, 76,
    79, 100, 111, 119, 138
Cane Creek Cotton Mill 76
Cane Creek Friends Meeting 34,
    36, 45, 47, 67, 82, 84, 91,
    108
Cantor, Jones 75
Carter, David 93
Carteret, John, Earl Granville 22
Carter family 21, 37, 41
Carter, Gilliam 117
Carter, John 39
Chamness 148
Chamness family 21

Chamness, William 106
Chatham County 22, 113, 115,
    118, 119
Chavis, John 79
Chavis, Peter 79
Civil War 14, 15, 41, 42, 60, 66,
    81, 82, 91, 108, 111, 114,
    117, 118, 119, 120, 121
Clark, Grady 126, 127
Clark, John Carrol "Cap" 128
Clark, Oliver 126, 127
Clover Orchard Store 79
Cobb, Elmo 143
Coble, Claude 84
Coble, Claude and Bessie 84
Coble, Elizabeth 64
Coble, Finley 94, 108
Coble, Floyd 80
Coble, John 75
Coble, Milton 68
Coble, Stanley 75, 119
Coble Store 80
colored school 138
Coltrane, Darold (Darryl) 98
Coltrane, Delacey 98
Coltrane, Milton 98
Coltrane, William 97
Company Shops 104
Compton, Phyllis 97
Confederates 117
Cornwallis, Lord Charles 51, 53
Councilman, George 112
Cox, Isham 88
Cox, Jennie 71
Croker, William 79
Crooks, Adam 111, 113

D

Dicks, Zachariah 39
Dixon, Cicero 94
Dixon, Diner (Dinah?) 79
Dixon, Elizabeth Allen 23
Dixon, Ernest P. 134
Dixon, Eula Louise 78, 84
Dixon, Gurney 82
Dixon, Hugh 76, 82, 112
Dixon, Jennie 82
Dixon, Joe 78
Dixon, Mahlon 93
Dixon, Simon 22, 50, 53, 54, 56,
    74, 75, 113
Dixon, Thomas C. 76, 93, 108
dressage 131
Duncan, French 126, 127
Durham, Charlie 81
Durham, Coy 126
Durham, John 81

E

Easterling, Gary 98
Edwards, Baker 117
Eli Whitney 15, 67, 89, 128, 134,
    136
Eli Whitney School 134
Engold, Edmond 68
Evans, Shubal 64, 66

F

Fairmount Foundry 81
Fanning, Colonel David 59
Fanning, Edmund 46, 48
farming 73
Faust, Peter 120

Flint Hill 93
Floyd Coble's Store 84
Fogleman, Bill 78
Fogleman, Brad 144
Fogleman, Lewis 126, 127
Foust, Albert 93
Foust, Allen 79
Foust, Patty 98
Fox, Anne 125
Freedom's Hill Wesleyan Church
    105, 108, 111, 114, 115
Frye, Katrine 125

G

Gilliam, Ed 126
Gilliam, James 119
Gowings, Hinton 79
Graham 15, 81, 82, 96, 129, 131,
    143
Graham, Allen 126, 127
Great Wagon Road 20
Green, Callie 34
Griffin, Cleo 35
Griffin, James 81
Griffin, Larry 36
Griffin, Lorraine 84
Griffin, Wilma 84
Guthrie, Alfred 117
Guthrie, Clabourn 107
Guthrie, Eleanor Newlin 76
Guthrie, Jim 107

H

Hackney, Myrtle Love 84
Hadley, Ann Long 41
Hammer, Jane Allen 94
Hammer Memorial School 94

Hanford, Callie Green 84
Hargrove, Hal 42
Harris, Wesley 117
Harvey, Kay 98
Hathcock, Ned 79
Hawfields 19, 20, 41, 54, 60, 78, 100, 127
Haw Fields 31
Helton (Hilton), John 120
Henley, William 81
Hinshaw, Willie B. and Lola 96
Holladay family 23
Holliday family 37, 41
Holliday, Henry 21
Holman family 76
Holman Mill 76
Holt Mills 76
Hornaday, T.H. 78
Hornady, Balaam 68
hunters 117
Husband, Herman 21, 46, 49, 50
Husbands, Mary 79
Husbans, Herman 45

I

Isely, Ralph 93

J

John Allen House 25
Johnson family 69
Johnson, Harry 126, 127
Johnson, Jardie 126
Johnson, William 119
Jones, Dean 142
Jones family 21
Jones, Starr 142

K

Kane, William 21
Kemp family 21
Kimball, Kyle 35
Kimball, Sarah 5
Kimball, Will 35, 73
Kimrey, William 89
Kirkman House 108, 112
Kirkman, William 108

L

Laton, Sherman 126
Laughlin family 21, 37
Laughlin, Hugh 75
Liberty 127
Lil John's Mountain Music 18, 139, 143
Lindley, Annie 89
Lindley, Bill 126
Lindley family 37, 41
Lindley, Joe Bill and Jane 74
Lindley, Jonathan 40
Lindley, Jonathon 54
Lindley's Mill 23, 45, 52, 60, 75
Lindley's Mill, Battle of 39, 59
Lindley, Thomas 21, 74
Lindley, William 40
Little Ward Mill 75
Lohr, Lawrence 127
Loyalists 52
Loy, Solomon 82
Luterlow, Ellen 117
Luterlow, Osage 117
Luterlow, Washington "Wash" 117

M

Maness, Jeff 139
Maness, Joel 139
Maness, "Lil" John, II 139
Maness, Pat 139
Marlet, Hannah 42
Marshall, William and Rebecca 32
Martin family 21
Matthews, Marilyn 36
Matthews, Neil 144
May, Benjamin 66
McBane, Burton 84
McBane, Nannie 136
McBane, Perisho 42
McPherson, Caleb 84
McPherson family 23
McPherson, John 68
McPherson, Lesa 36
McPherson, Micajah 112, 115, 117
McPherson, Mrs. Patton 69
McPherson, Phoebe 117
McPherson, Sam 79
McVey, Harris 81
McVey, Monroe 36
McVey, Thomas 78
Millstone Catering 133
Moon, Cletus 72
Moon, Dacie 110, 114
Morgan, Pat 72
Murcheson, Tim 128
Murchison, Mary 64
Murchison, W.G. 66

N

Newlin, Algie 37, 126
Newlin, Elbert 34
Newlin family 37, 41
Newlin, James 119
Newlin, John 106
Newlin, Nathaniel 107
Newlin, Oliver 106
Newlin, Thomas 107
Newlin, William 119
North Carolina State Baseball
    Championship 127

O

Orange County 20, 21, 22, 49, 76,
    89, 103
Original Hollywood Horror Show
    18, 142
Overground Railroad 106
Overman, Andrew and Virginia 67
Overman, Henry J. 67
Overman, John 75, 86
Owens, William 120

P

Pathway to Freedom 18, 137
Patterson, Dennis 98
Pennsylvania 50, 74, 75
Perry, Clay 126
Perry, Glen 128
Perry, Joe 126
Perry, Leland 126
Pickard, Leroy 69
Pickard, Margaret and Daniel 76
Pike, Abigail 32
Pike family 21, 23
Pike, Janet 125
Pike, John 70
Pike, Moses 93
Pike, Mr. and Mrs. Joe 71
Pike, William 68

plank road 82
Pleasant Hill Christian Church 63, 121, 138
Pleasant Hill Temperance Society 99
Pleasant Union Wesleyan Church 69
Porter, John 36
pottery 82
Pyle, Dr. John 45, 52, 61
Pyle, John 54
Pyle's Hacking Match 53
Pyle's Massacre 39, 52

Q

Quakenbush, Seton 126
Quakers 14, 18, 20, 21, 23, 31, 32, 34, 35, 37, 39, 40, 41, 42, 45, 46, 48, 49, 50, 51, 52, 53, 60, 61, 63, 91, 100, 105, 106, 107, 109, 111, 117, 118, 119, 126, 129, 130, 137, 139, 143

R

Randolph Coble House 29
Randolph, John 110
Regulator Movement 46
Regulators 48, 49, 54
Regulators Revolt 45
Revolutionary War 14, 39, 40, 45, 51, 59, 62, 68, 74, 137
Roach, James 84
Roach, Monroe 71, 116
Robbins, L.B. 69
Roberson, Robert Eugene "Rob" 139
Roberson, Sallie 78
Rock Creek United Methodist Church 68

Ruth, J. Wesley 71
Ruth, O.L. 71

S

Saxapahaw 107
schools 41, 64, 88, 89, 91, 94, 95, 96, 98, 125, 126, 127, 128, 134, 135, 136, 138, 139, 143
  Bethel 89
  Cane Creek 88
  "colored" 96
  Fogleman 87
  Hunting Branch 87
  Kimrey 89
  Oak Dale Academy 89
  Oak Dale High 89
  Oak Springs 88
  Patterson 89
  Pinefield 89
  Pleasant Hill 88, 89
  Sandy Grove 88
  West Point 87
Scotten, Lewis 76
Shoffner, Ernest 98
Shoffner, Floyd 98
Shoffner, Mark 98
slavery 40, 103, 105, 108
Snow Camp Foundry and Machine Shops 79
Snow Camp Manufacturing Company 79
Snow Camp Milling Company 81
Snow Camp Mutual Telephone Company 84
Snow Camp Outdoor Theatre 17, 21, 95, 96, 136
Snow Camp Raygo 17, 84
Snow Camp Roller Mill 81

Snow Camp Woolen Mill 15, 76, 78, 81
Sourwood Forest Golf Club 143
Sourwood Golf Course 18
Spray, Reverend Howard 68
Spring Friends Meeting 21, 37, 61, 106, 118, 119, 126, 130, 134
Stafford, Nathan 81
Staley, Martin 63, 88
Staley, Sandra 98
Stearns, Shubal 31, 38
Stephens, P.H. 35
Stephens, Simon 91
Stockard, Sallie 78
Stockard, Sally 105
Stockard, W.J. 81
Stout, Charlie 35
Stout family 23
Stout, Flora 93
Stout, Harry 126, 127
Stout, Peter 76
Stout, Rachel 25
Stout, Tommy 125
Stout, William P. 35
Stout, William Patterson 82, 84
Stuart, Amos 118
Stuart, Ed 84
Stuart, Jehu 47
Stuart, Odie 35
Swing, G. Talmadge 69
Sword of Peace, The 18, 136, 137
Sydnor, Cindy 131
Sydnor, Eliza 132
Sylvan Academy 87
Sylvan of the Grove Academy 91
Sylvan School 15, 18, 34, 35, 72, 82, 91, 94, 95, 97, 98, 108, 125, 126, 128, 139

T

tanners 82
Tate, Sam 93
teacherage 95
Teague, Bobbie 36, 96
Teague, Christopher 66
Teague, David 70
Teague, E.M. 75
Teague family 69
Teague, Marion 73
Teague, Marjorie 103
Teague, Swannie 84
Teague, York 138
Terry, Thomas B. 71
Thomas, James 120
Thompson, Aaron 79
Thompson, David 84
Thompson family 23
Thompson, Gabe 79
Thompson, Hayes 34
Thompson, John 76
Thompson, Karen 95, 134
Thompson, Lannie 35
Thompson, Lattie 138
Thompson, Lucy 93
Thompson Mill 75
Thompson, Paul 72, 86
Thompson, Ray 86
Thompson's Garage 86
Thompson, William 75
Tidwell family 21
Tinnen, Hiram 79
Tiny, H.J. 84
Tyson, Susanna 64

U

Uncle Eli's Quilting Party 134
Underground Railroad 103, 109, 112
Unthank, Temple 81

V

Vestal, Alfred 112

W

Walls, George 11, 96, 134
Ward, Charlie 76
Ward, Stephen 75
War Quakers 118
Way, A.H. 66
Way, A.M. 65, 88
Way, Benjamin 75
Way, Celia 64
Way, Donnie 87, 138, 139
Weaver, John 79
Weaver, Wesley 79
Wells family 21
Whitehead, Dolph 35
White, Isah (Isaiah) 79
White, Sheila 98
Wicker, Floyd Euliss 128
Williams, Earl 126
Williams, Margaret 112
Wilson, Bryan 133
Wilson, James and Louise 133
Wilson, Mike 139
Wilson, Robert and Ruby 133
Wolfe, Floyd 142
Wolfe Wines 141
Woody, Ellen and Martha 42
Woody family 23, 37, 41

Workman, Alex 72
Workman, Jesse 76
Wrenn, Henry C. 71
Wright, Charity 47
Wright family 21, 69
Wright, Gertrude and Julius 70
Wright, Nathan 35
Wright, Rachel 32

Y

Ye Olde Country Kitchen 17, 133
Yesterday's Grill 17, 133, 134

Z

Zachary, Alfred L. and Ila Guthrie 129
Zachary family 23
Zachary, George 126
Zachary, James 117
Zachary, Seymore 117
Zachary, Tom 126, 129

ABOUT THE AUTHOR

Tim Allen, along with his wife, Jackie, lives on a small horse farm in Snow Camp. While a minister, he began writing and published professional articles and three devotional books, *Seasons in the Year*, *When the Season Is Dry* and *Mothers Around the Manger*, all from Smyth & Helwys. He wrote a weekly column for the *Henderson Daily Dispatch* in the mid-1990s and later contributed articles to *Alamance Magazine*. Allen has written several series of Sunday school lessons for Smyth & Helwys, published academic articles on early American religious history in *North Carolina Historical Review* and *Methodist History* and has entries in the online encyclopedia North Carolina History Project. His book *North Carolina Quakers: Spring Friends Meeting* was published by Arcadia Press in 2011. His degrees are in religious studies (BA and MA), divinity (MDiv) and theological studies (PhD). Allen has taught at Louisburg College, Vance-Granville Community College, Randolph Community College and the University of North Carolina–Greensboro. Currently, he teaches humanities for Strayer University and the University of Phoenix, as well as biblical studies for the Graduate Theological Foundation. When not teaching and writing, he enjoys music, guitars and doing sound work for bands and festivals.